SHADOW TIME STORIES

D1557233

Lilo Beil

Translated by: Virginia C. Larsen

Cover Illustration:
Max Liebermann (1847 – 1935) *The Granddaughter, Writing (1923)*

Originally published in German:
© 2005 Edition Tintenfass
69239 Neckarsteinach
Germany
Tel/Fax:49-62 29-23 22
www.verlag-tintenfass-de
info@verlag-tintenfass.de

ISBN: 1530392810
ISBN 13: 9781530392810

SHADOW
TIME STORIES

*Wahrheit und Imagination sind wie zwei Schwestern, die
Arm in Arm daherkommen.*
*-- Lilo Beil (Truth and imagination are like two sisters,
who come walking up together.)*

Ikh gleyb in der zun, afile ven zi shaynt nisht;
Ikh gleyb in der libe, afile ven ikh fil zi nisht;
Ikh gleyb in Got, afile ven er shvaygt.
I believe in the sun, even when it doesn't shine;
I believe in love, even when I don't feel it;
I believe in God, even when He is silent.
Jewish inscription on the wall of a cellar in Cologne
in which Jews were hidden during the Holocaust.

AUTHOR'S
INTRODUCTION

I have often been asked why I wrote about the Third Reich although I didn't experience those 12 horrible years of Hitler's dictatorship myself.

I was born in 1947, two years after the end of World War II, daughter of a Protestant pastor in the Southern Palatinate near the border separating Germany from Alsatia and Northern France.

I spent my childhood and teen years with my younger sister, Marianne, in one of the most idyllic parsonages one can imagine. It was built in the age of Goethe and was surrounded by an extensive garden.

The 1950s and '60s were known as the Adenauer era, characterized by conservatism and the so-called *Wirtschaftswunder* (economic boom). This era saw the general rise in living standard of the populace, thanks to its industrious character, but it was also marked by silence and repression of its most recent past. No one wanted to be reminded of the horrors of the war and their own part in it (whether active or passive).

I have processed a pivotal experience from my own childhood in the story "Twilight Hour." The little girl, Margaret, happens to overhear a conversation between her parents about the Holocaust. I am that Margaret, and still today as an adult I consider that moment to be the end of my childhood innocence.

All of the stories in this book spring from my feeling of utter incomprehension, sadness and fury over what occurred in my country before my birth. The hardest to acknowledge is that the perpetrators, the collaborators, and the silently acquiescent were entirely normal human beings, not monsters. Hannah Arendt, the great German-Jewish philosopher, calls this phenomenon "the banality of evil."

Until the end of my life, I will remain unable to comprehend what happened in Germany during the

Nazi dictatorship. But I am just as incredulous over the atrocities which continue to be perpetrated the world over.

In my stories, I have tried to depict the daily cruelties which preceded the Holocaust and the gradual exclusion of people who did not fit into the Nazis' fanatical picture of an ideal world.

To be sure, there were small gestures of humanity among the German people, many of whom became victims themselves of tyranny. Some of my stories reveal the better side of human nature during this "time of shadows," a time I hope we will never have to experience again.

TRANSLATOR'S NOTE

In 2007, I visited the village of Rimbach, Germany, a short distance north of Heidelberg and south of Frankfurt, where I had taught English and French years before at the Martin-Luther-Schule. One of the teachers, Jutta Meyer, gave me a book to read on the plane back to Minnesota. It was *Schattenzeit Geschichten* (*Shadow Time Stories*), written by a woman named Lilo Beil, who had also taught English and French at the M-L-S, arriving two years after my departure.

I was deeply stirred by the stories of people young and old living in German villages during Hitler's rise to power. I saw how Nazi propaganda affected (infected!) the interactions of Germans and Jews in these semi-rural settings between 1937 and 1945. It was frustrating that I couldn't share these stories with my friends at home because they didn't speak or read German.

I wrote to Lilo Beil to tell her what an impact her stories had had on me. We ended up as the email equivalent of pen-pals (e-pals?), and eventually I asked her if I might translate this book. She was delighted and very moved. This translation is my contribution to Lilo's ceaseless efforts to promote understanding, acceptance, and nurturing among people of different ethnic origins. She discusses certain stories with German school children and gives book readings in villages and cities, mostly in her native region between Rimbach and the French border province of Alsace.

I am indebted to my spouse Kirsten Lindbloom for doing all of the technical work associated with publishing and to our dear friend Jocelyn Pihlaja for her fine-tooth editing. I wish to pay tribute to Deb Rentfrow, who began as my publishing and tech assistant but succumbed to a quick, aggressive return of her cancer. She helped me over the initial legal hurdles and believed strongly in the worth of my project.

Virginia Larsen
Austin, Minnesota
March 2016

CONTENTS

SHADOW TIME

May. Finally, it was May. That meant it was almost summer.

Elisabeth didn't really start to live until May arrived. There were certain signs, like the elderberry bushes would have to blossom creamy-white along the garden walls and the border around the fields and in the clearing in the woods. The poppies would have to decorate the sparse patches of earth on the rubbish heaps, and her favorite tree with its leafy canopy would invite her to read and dream.

Elisabeth had agreed to meet her friend Cosima at four o'clock. Four o'clock at their favorite tree - because tomorrow was Mother's Day.

Every year their mothers said the same thing, "Please don't buy any gifts; we prefer something you made yourselves - a picture or maybe a bouquet of meadow flowers you each picked and arranged yourself. That makes us much happier than some silly thing you bought in a store."

That's what Elisabeth's mother, Frau Kern, and Cosima's mother, Frau Oppenheimer, said every year to their daughters, who were Very Best Friends. As though they had memorized the same words.

All right, Elisabeth thought, as she waited for Cosima, some hand-picked wild flowers. Wild baby's breath, buttercups (which turned your nose yellow when you sniffed them), something blue, if possible....

In addition, Cosima had said something about a secret, but it was maybe not a very good secret because Cosima, usually the merry one, hadn't looked so merry when she spoke of it.

Cosima, Elisabeth thought, was truly a puzzling creature. There was always something new to discover about her. Her whole family was that way. Cosima's parents were musicians in the city theatre. Her mother sang in the chorus, and her father played first violin in the orchestra. The Oppenheimers were "Wagnerians", said Elisabeth's parents. That meant they were admirers of the great composer Richard Wagner and his music. The Wagnerian operas were, one could say, very "Germanic." Elisabeth's parents didn't care for that very much, but the Oppenheimers, who were Jewish, loved the heroic and fairy tale aspects and the mysterious music, which many people simply did not understand.

In honor of the great composer, both Oppenheimer children were named, logically, Richard, after Richard Wagner, and Cosima, after Cosima Wagner, the composer's wife. The two plump cats, one orange and the other black, were named Kriemhilda and Brunhilda, after the queens in the Nibelungen legend. The little black cuddly dog was named Alberich after the guardian of the Nibelungen treasure.

"The Oppenheimers are so witty and humorous, not like the others who live in our street. They're all so straight-laced," said Elisabeth's parents. It wasn't just the girls who were friends; the grown-ups got together often as well.

There was always laughter at the Oppenheimers' house, and at Elisabeth's house, too. But lately the grown-up talk was more often serious. They talked about the man with the moustache, the "rat-catcher." He was the one who always screamed and carried on when his speeches were broadcast on the radio. In the beginning, the grown-ups made fun of the "screeching monkey" or the "no-talent picture paint-er" as they called him. And they had said, "Nobody is going to take that fellow seriously...."

However, there were elections, and the screech-ing monkey was elected. Not only that: people were enthusiastic about him.

Elisabeth and Cosima didn't understand any of that very well. Nor did they understand the expres-sion on the faces of their parents when the man with the moustache yelled on the radio. What business was it of theirs anyway? All of that was politics, and politics belonged to the world of adults just like earn-ing money, saving money, worrying about the future, and other unpleasant things.

As long as May arrived on schedule, as long as Elisabeth and Cosima were able to sit in the branch-es of their favorite tree, and as long as there were meadow flowers which they could tie into a bouquet for Mother's Day, then the world was safe. Brown rat-catchers and yelling men with moustaches were simply not allowed near their favorite tree and elderberry-bordered meadows and fields. Grown-ups could talk about politics as much as they wanted; the children would ignore it all.

It was already a quarter after four when Cosima came rushing up. Cosima with the braids blonde as wheat and the cornflower blue eyes. She was out of breath and had to sit and pant for a moment after hoisting herself up onto the limb next to Elisabeth.

"Your secret?" asked Elisabeth, going straight to the point.

"We're busy packing and I had to help. Grand-mother has sent us enough money so that we can leave the country. Our papers are here, too. So it's final. We're leaving."

Elisabeth didn't understand any of this and thought Cosima was just kidding. Sometimes Cosima told fibs just because her head was so full of wild ideas.

"Where are you going?" Elisabeth asked, aghast, for somehow this didn't seem like something Cosima was making up.

"We're going to live with my grandmother in Boston. That's in America, you know."

"How come so far away? And immediately? And to America!"

"Well, it's because of the 'Brown Rat-Catcher.' You know, the 'Screeching Monkey.' And it's because of the Aryan race, whatever that is. We're not Aryan, not Germanic like regular Germans. Like you, for example, you and your family."

"But your name is Cosima, and your brother's is Richard, and you've got Kriemhilda and Brunhilda, the cats, and Alberich, the dog. They must be one hundred percent Germanic, and your parents are Wagnerians and love everything Germanic and...."

Here Cosima interrupted with a laugh and said, "...and none of that means anything. It doesn't matter at all to the 'Brown Rat-Catcher' and his men. My parents said so. That's why we have to leave."

Cosima continued quite soberly. "My grandmother in Boston wrote that these men will stop at nothing. She said in her letter, 'You absolutely must get out of Germany; otherwise you will end up caught in a trap.' She told us what the American newspapers were reporting." Cosima said that was why they were leaving the very next day: they feared for their lives!

Elisabeth tried to be brave. It was very hard. "I envy you a little bit. You'll get to know the land of Tom Sawyer and Huckleberry Finn. Maybe you can travel down the Mississippi on one of those fantastic paddle wheel boats. You won't need to read any more Karl May novels because you'll see real Indians and cowboys. You…." She fell silent.

Cosima said, "Oh, I don't care much about cowboys and Indians - I'd rather stay in the land of Lorelei and Tom Thumb and the gingerbread witch. But we can't; we have to leave. My parents call it *emigrating*. We've still got some things to organize…." She paused, then went on. "We aren't allowed to take animals on board the ship. Do you think you could…?"

"Of course!" Elisabeth was quick to reassure her. "Alberich, Kriemhilda and Brunhilda will be welcome at our house. I'm sure my parents will say it's all right. You know that I have the best parents in the world - along with yours, of course."

Then they leapt from the limb of their favorite tree and began to pick wild flowers for two gigantic Mother's Day bouquets.

It was a picture-perfect day in May, and that's when the "shadow time" began.

THE SAILOR DRESS

I t was getting colder.

Already the birds were gathering in flocks, getting ready to fly south. One by one they came to perch on the telephone wires, until the wires were black with them. The fields had been harvested and were now bare. The wind whistled across the stubble and stripped the trees bare. Before long winter would arrive, and it would be Christmas-time.

Lisa stood in front of the tiny shop's display window. There it was, the dark blue dress with a white sailor collar. It had light blue piping and a stitched-on pocket on each side. She remembered seeing it recently when she and Mother came into the city. Mother had an appointment with the dentist.

Lisa was sure Herr Loewenstein would have put the dress away for winter. Yet there it was!

But yearning for it was a sin. It was a sin and plainly forbidden. The teacher had said so, and the teacher knew everything. Lisa was able to multiply one-times-one forward and backward. Even sideways. She knew how to write "noxious" and "vermin", which referred to certain people, who were also labeled "enemies of Germany." She knew how high the Alpine Zugspitze was and also the Obersalzberg mountain. She knew it all, and she also knew that it would be a sin to buy a dress in this shop.

"Do not buy anything from Jews," the teacher had said. She had even written the sentence on the board and had underlined it with yellow chalk. Frieda Huber, the smartest pupil and also the teacher's pet, was picked to read the sentence to the class three times in a loud voice.

Only three days after seeing the dress again, a special visitor appeared at Lisa's home. It was Uncle Rudolf. He was her father's older brother who had emigrated to America many years ago as a young man. That was long before Lisa was born. Now he was back in Westfalia to visit his family and see his birthplace again.

Uncle Rudolf had been quite successful in the "New World," as the grown-ups often called it. He owned a thriving butcher shop in a suburb of Chicago. It was maybe even bigger and better than the one owned by Lisa's parents. He had brought along a lot of photos. After closing time, the whole family gathered around the dining table, and he passed around the photos to be admired. Everyone was very proud of Uncle Rudolf.

Uncle was friendly and good-natured and generous. For Lisa and her two brothers, he had brought splendid toys. There were two "real" teddy bears for the boys. One had a dark red velvet ribbon tied in a bow around its neck, and the other had a light blue bow. Lisa received a doll that said some words in English when she pressed its tummy. For her younger brother, there was a wind-up elephant, and for her older brother two brightly painted miniature cars. Not only that: Uncle Rudolf would delve into one of his checkered suitcases and produce sweets that they had never seen or tasted before - brown toffees and something he called "chocolate." They tasted heavenly. Surely America must be a paradise for children since it was full of so many different kinds of sweets.

Sadly, Uncle Rudolf was leaving soon to return to America. It would be a long voyage on an enormous ocean steamer. Lisa would gladly have gone with him because he had told countless exciting stories about gold diggers and Indians with colorful feather headdresses and painted faces. He had told them about "skyscrapers," buildings so high it made people dizzy just to look up at them, and about huge waterfalls and about trees so big that ten grown men couldn't get their arms around even one of them. And finally about the fantastic wild animals living in the desert.

Lisa had become very excited about his stories, but she did not repeat any of them at school. When she had first told the teacher about Uncle Rudolf's visit, the teacher had made a face. Her mouth became a tight, thin, crooked line whenever she was annoyed. "The Americans always print such dreadful things about Germany in their newspapers. Nothing but lies and exaggerations," she said.

Surely it was a sin even to wish to go to America with Uncle Rudolf, and so she didn't mention her American uncle and his wonderful land at school anymore.

Uncle Rudolf had said to Lisa, "I want you to pick out one more thing before I leave, something really beautiful. That will be your early Christmas present.

Who knows when I'll be able to come back for another visit?" Uncle's face was very serious when he said this. Lisa didn't know why - he certainly could afford to come back to Germany again.

Now here they were, standing in front of Herr Loewenstein's shop. The sailor dress was still in the window. It was very, very beautiful even though it was a sin to buy anything from Herr Loewenstein because he belonged to the category of "noxious vermin" and "enemies of the people."

The teacher had made it very plain: Germans should not buy anything from such people.

Lisa repeated the teacher's words to Uncle Rudolf, who became very angry and said: "Nonsense. Utter nonsense! Such rubbish! Has everybody here gone crazy? I am an American, and I choose to buy something here. End of discussion." She had never before heard her good-natured uncle talk like that. He then marched straight up the steps to the shop's entrance. Lisa followed him hesitantly.

Then they were standing in the shop. They were the only customers. Herr Loewenstein, short and bent over and with a face full of wrinkles, fetched the dress from the display window. It fit Lisa perfectly and went well with her page-boy haircut. Uncle Rudolf paid at the cash register.

"Thank you, sir," said Herr Lowenstein. His eyes looked very sad. "You are an American? God bless you, sir." And to Lisa he said in a warm voice, "Enjoy your new dress, little girl." Lisa looked embarrassed. Her cheeks reddened, and she bit her lip.

She was sure the teacher didn't know Herr Loewenstein personally; otherwise she would not have called certain people "noxious vermin." Could it be that the teacher was lying? Lisa's head was full of conflicting thoughts.

Uncle took the shopping bag with the sailor dress, and the two of them left the shop. With his ancient, sad eyes, Herr Loewenstein watched them go.

That evening, before bedtime, Lisa put on the sailor dress again. She turned this way and that in front of the mirror and examined her reflection carefully. Everything seemed to be in order. She didn't notice anything conspicuous. She hoped that neither the teacher nor her classmates would suspect where the dress came from.

A sudden chilling gust of wind blew in through the window and frightened her. The curtain ballooned, sending several school notebooks skidding off her desk and onto the floor. She closed the window. Then, very slowly, she took off the sailor dress and folded it carefully. She placed it on the top shelf in her closet. She wondered, as she did so, if she would have the courage to wear the dress next spring. Maybe. Or maybe not.

She would have to sleep on it.

LEA'S JOURNEY TO
THE EAST

Her mother had dressed her in the little red coat that she dearly loved. It went so well with her black patent leather shoes and white knee socks.

"Why are we going on a trip anyway? And where to?" Lea had asked. "It's just the beginning of May, and summer vacation isn't until July!"

"We are going to the East," Mother had answered.

That had sounded very nice. There were echoes of the Baltic and summer breezes and striped beach umbrellas and beach balls, of eating ice cream and building sand castles, and not only that but the sun also rose every morning in the East. They had been there once, for the whole vacation, Father, Mother and Lea.

But Mother's voice was different today. No hint of sun, wind or children's laughter. Instead, it sounded very serious. In many ways, lately her lovely, elegant mother had become unusually quiet. She seemed distracted and oppressed. Lea told herself that things would surely improve when Father came back from this long business trip. He had left for the East, very suddenly. He hadn't even been able to say goodbye properly to his wife and daughter.

Several months before that, some children she barely knew and even some of her schoolmates had begun to point at her and whisper among themselves. They avoided her on the playground. Except for Anna. Anna told her not to pay any attention to them. They were stupid, she said.

Lately, in the shops, Lea and her mother were treated coolly. Nice Frau Krause, who owned the grocery store on the corner, was the exception. She continued to tuck in a few of Lea's favorite hard candies, the bright red raspberry ones, which felt so sparkly on her tongue. But Frau Krause only did this when no one else was in the store.

All of that was somehow connected to the "brown men," as Lea's mother called them, because of their uniforms, and with the yellow star which Lea's family were obliged to wear now whenever they left the house.

Lea picked up her smart little patent leather suitcase, which Father had given her last year on her ninth birthday. In the other hand, she carried Klara, her favorite doll, a present from her friend Anna, who lived on the same floor.

Anna and Lea had taken ballet lessons together in a city near their village. The previous winter, Anna and Lea had danced in *The Nutcracker* with their class. Lea had starred as Klara; Anna was the Nutcracker.

The ballet master had insisted that Lea be allowed to remain in the group even though she was "not Aryan." She was the most talented dancer and he had "connections upstairs," whatever that meant.

For Christmas, Lea had given Anna a splendid hand-carved Nutcracker. It was painted in bright colors and gleamed in the light.

Anna had delighted Lea with her gift: a Klara doll. Klara had springy corkscrew curls tied up in a satin bow.

Now, when Lea stepped into the stairwell with her mother, Anna was standing in front of her apartment door with the Nutcracker in her hand. Anna had remained her friend in spite of the brown-clad men and the yellow star. As she stood at the door, Anna looked at them, wide-eyed and serious.

"We are going on a journey," said Lea. "To the East. I think it is better for Klara to stay here with you." And she handed the doll with the blonde corkscrew curls to Anna. "Take good care of her until I come back."

"I promise," answered Anna softly. Neither of them knew yet that the "shadow time" had begun.

WHEN THEY KILLED
THE CHRIST CHILD

Luisa's father was a pastor in a little village not far from the French border. They lived in a big, old house with many high-ceilinged rooms, bay windows and niches, with a wide stairway that had a coconut-fiber runner to protect it, and a brass handrail.

The stairs led to a balcony in the corner of which a swing was mounted. A little, winding staircase led further into an attic full of adventuresome possibilities. Spider webs hung from the ceiling like ghosts. Chests and trunks contained treasures galore: dresses, hats, walking canes, stockings, kerchiefs, high-heeled shoes, lacy gloves, bags, purses and pouches, shawls and cloaks, all good for disguises and acting out stories on days when it was not possible to play in the garden.

The roof tiles were two-hundred-years old and supported a stork nest that was still inhabited. The garden was large and had gotten a bit out of hand. There was a bower and some dense shrubbery, some fruit trees and a boxwood-lined path.

Luisa's best friend was Judith Mandelbaum. Her parents ran a little grocery store. It was not very profitable because the people living in the village were mostly self-sufficient. After all, it was a farming community.

Luisa admired Judith, who was good at arithmetic and who didn't mind helping her with her homework. Judith was also good in German. Her penmanship was precise and beautiful, and she could memorize anything quick as a wink. Not only that, but she could retain everything much longer than Luisa, who, to be honest, was only really good at drawing and painting. They had to learn poems by heart, like "The Pledge", and "The Bell", and "The Glove", and "The Elf King", and "The Guarantee", and "The Feet in the Fire", poems which all German pupils had been memorizing for generations. Luisa agonized. It was child's play for Judith.

Judith wasn't only smarter than Luisa, she was also prettier. Luisa was rather chubby, with red cheeks, blue eyes and long blonde braids. She hated her apple-cheeks and pink skin; she hated being blonde - it was boring. And she hated her upturned nose.

Judith was always olive-complexioned, even in winter. In summer, her skin darkened even more, so different from Luisa, who turned red as a lobster after even a brief exposure to the sun.

Judith had the most beautiful hair that Luisa had ever seen, thick and long and shiny black. Judith's nose was delicate and slightly curved, very noble-looking, and her mouth was like ripe cherries.

The other village children made fun of Judith in school, called her "the black one" and wouldn't let her play with them during recess. They yelled hateful names when her back was turned and never invited her over to their houses to play.

Recently, the grown-ups of the village stopped buying groceries from Judith's parents. The children became meaner and meaner to Judith - because they didn't know any better: they imitated their parents, whom they were supposed to obey anyway. Lately they looked sideways at her in religion class, which was taught by Luisa's father - even though Judith had been baptized like all the others.

Luisa's father called on Judith frequently because she knew such a lot; it seemed as if she might know all of Biblical history by heart. Difficult names like Abimelech, Bathsheba, Zerrubbabel, Zachariah, Ahasuerus, Absalom, Naomi and Obadiah she pronounced as easily as other children said names like Otto, Karl, Paul and Werner. Luisa's father often used Judith as a good example, but that made the other children angry. They were envious.

Because of that, Luisa's father soon received an anonymous letter telling him to kick the "black one" out of religion class and stop favoring her over the German children.

It was signed "A well-meaning Christian woman."

Luisa's father tore up the letter in anger and hissed, "This bad lot of brown uniforms. They are making things worse and worse, even here in our village." In the following weeks, he seemed rather uncomfortable in religion class and called on Judith less often than before.

Luisa started playing less and less often with Judith although she didn't want to admit that she was taking her cue from the others. She stopped asking

Judith for help with her homework, and her grades began to slip in all subjects except art.

"The Brown Shirts are becoming bolder and more disrespectful than ever," said Luisa's father, but he only said this at home, within his own four walls, and sometimes he even went to the door to make sure the hired girl wasn't eavesdropping.

"The walls have ears," said Mother.

"They send these fellows to church every Sunday. There they sit with their fresh young faces, their impudent grins and their brown uniforms, just waiting for me to say the wrong thing. Recently, when I preached on the Beatitudes and said that we should love our neighbor whether he is white, brown or yellow, I saw them poke each other in the ribs, and one fellow took out his notebook and wrote something down. Since then, I haven't felt free to speak the way I'd like to." Luisa's father fell silent. Lately, he seemed sad and worried, and she noticed with a start that his hair was starting to turn gray.

Christmas was approaching. In religion class, the pupils fashioned a miniature manger. The boys constructed the little Bethlehem stable with great enthusiasm and carved small animals of soft wood: ox, donkey, sheep. They also carved the Holy Three

Kings, Kaspar, Melchior and Balthasar, along with the shepherds and angels and the Holy Family. The girls were responsible for the details. They painted the primitive wooden figures, fetched straw and hay and made a glowing star out of gold foil to hang above the stable.

Fritz and Helmut Kottmann, sons of the local political leader, elbowed each other on the sly as soon as they saw that Judith was the one chosen to paint the Christ child. Luisa's father had simply pressed the Christ child into her hand. A slight shadow passed over Judith's face, and when she said "Thank you," her voice quavered a little.

Her classmates, Hilde, Gertrud, Erika and Elfriede, had looked over at her, nearly green with envy. Judith painted and painted. She lost track of time, and she forgot the awful smell of paste wax in the stuffy schoolroom and the disgruntled looks coming from all sides.

Finally Judith walked up to Luisa's father, seated at his desk. She carried something carefully in her outstretched hands.

The Christ child was finished, but it was a strange-looking Christ child indeed. He had a little golden star on his bare chest, a teeny, tiny one just like the bigger one that Judith, her parents and some other people in the village had recently been obliged to wear, like the cattle dealer Mosche and his family, Max and Esther Hirschfeld, all of the Ellwangers and Abraham Menzel, the old musician.

Some of the children laughed and called out, "What in all the world is that supposed to mean? Such a stupid thing! Where does she get her ideas anyway? Is she trying to make fun of us?"

Luisa's father said, "Judith is right. Jesus was a Jew. We shouldn't forget that."

The very next day he received another letter, this one signed by a number of indignant German Christians.

Fritz and Helmut Kottmann sneaked into the schoolhouse that night and brought out Judith's Christ child. They built a fire behind their house and burned up the tiny figure with the gold star.

THE SUGAR BUNNY

It was springtime when Katharina learned the meaning of cowardice. She encountered cowardice not only in other people but also in herself. Katharina was ten years old, and her mother had asked her to run to the post office to mail a letter.

It was Easter Saturday. Mother was in a bad mood because she had so much work to do. Everything needed to be clean and sparkly for Easter dinner; lots of visitors were expected. There were cakes to bake, Easter eggs to dye, and the parlor to decorate. Critical aunts, uncles, and grandparents would examine Mother's domestic talents under a magnifying glass.

Katharina took the letter and hurried on her way, anxious to avoid a run-in with her crabby mother, the everlasting martyr. The sidewalks in front of all the houses in the village were swept regularly, and the flower boxes were full of boxwood and daffodils, tulips and narcissus. Some of the housewives scrubbed the door frames in front of their houses with bar soap. It was indeed a typical, that is to say, a very clean village in Southern Hessia. Katharina's mother would certainly beat out the competition in cleaning but then would vent her stress on her only child.

Across the street, behind the Golden Star restaurant, Katharina's friends Emma and Ilse were jumping rope while Ilse's little brothers played with clay marbles, which they called "clickers." Maybe the Easter bunny would bring glass marbles tomorrow, the kind with colored ribbons inside. Much more fun to play with them than with clickers.

"Come on over!" the two girls called.

"Can't! No time! Must run to the post office for Mother."

From Ilse's house came the aroma of baked sweet biscuits, used to make the Easter lambs which Ilse's mother made every year in huge quantities. It was a big family: eleven children. But Ilse never had to help because she was among the youngest. Her mother always seemed to be in a good mood, and Katharina couldn't help feeling envious.

Inside the post office, some seven people stood in line in front of the service window. The post office was about to close. Katharina took her place at the end of the line. This was going to take a while. The woman ahead of her turned around. It was Frau Rosenzweig.

Katharina was in the habit of paying Frau Rosenzweig a visit as often as her mother allowed because she had such wonderful books. Books, books, books, a paradise of books: *Leatherstocking Tales* and *The Last of the Mohicans*, children's classics like *The Nestling* by Ilse Ury, *Alice in Wonderland*, or *Heidi* and other books by Johanna Spyri, *Pinocchio* and *The Hunchback of Notre Dame.*

She always felt sorry for the hunchback of Notre Dame, poor man, made fun of and despised by everyone. She felt sorry for Esmeralda, too, the beautiful black-haired Gypsy with the glittering gold bracelets and earrings. Poor, unfortunate Esmeralda, who was dubbed a witch by mean people who wanted to catch and kill her.

These stories made Katharina sad because she didn't like it when bad things happened to nice people, especially to people who were helpless and alone. She also felt sorry for Don Quixote, who charged at windmills on his old bony horse, Rocinante. She didn't see the humor in such situations even though others laughed and tapped their foreheads.

But when the stories in Frau Rosenzweig's lovely books had a happy ending, when the bad ones were punished for their evil deeds and the good ones rewarded, then Katharina breathed a sigh of relief and wished fervently that real life could always be like that, too.

That is why she especially liked the stories of Charles Dickens: because poor Oliver Twist and David Copperfield came out on top even though they had to endure great hardships before justice prevailed.

Most of all she liked Frau Rosenzweig's fairy-tale books with their marvelous colored illustrations like *The German Treasury of Fairy-Tales*, a brand new book, huge, with shiny pictures. She also loved the tales of *A Thousand and One Nights*, told by the narrator, Sheherazade.

Frau Rosenzweig was also a kind of Sheherazade, for she excelled at telling fairy-tales. Frau Rosenzweig used to have a bookstore, but now she was over sixty and lived alone, without any family nearby, at the edge of town. Her little house had green shutters and was surrounded by fruit trees: plum, pears, peaches, and apples. Magnificent. Frau Rosenzweig had had a swing installed in the plum tree just for Katharina.

When Katharina went to Frau Rosenzweig's house recently to return a book, she noticed something next to the doorbell. Over the name-plate with "Sarah Rosenzweig" on it, somebody had scribbled "Jew-swine."

Katharina didn't understand the significance of what was written on Frau Rosenzweig's house, but it was ugly, and it made her shiver even though she was wearing a thick woolen vest. Frau Rosenzweig had tried to paint over the words, but their brown color shone through. It was a particularly stubborn color.

"A youngsters' prank," Frau Rosenzweig had said, glancing at the scribble and trying to sound nonchalant. But she had more creases in her forehead than usual, and Katharina noticed that her shoulders were stooped. She seemed very tired.

Now, at the post office, Frau Rosenzweig was feeling around in her large shopping basket. "This is good timing, Katharina. I was going to drop this off at your house." She gave Katharina a little package. Judging by the shape, it was a rabbit.

Every year for Easter, Frau Rosenzweig gave Katharina a bunny made of red sugar. Katharina loved these red sugar-bunnies - they glowed like lamps when held up to the light, either sunlight or candle-light, like the lamps in Frau Rosenzweig's books, like Aladdin's magic lamp, for example.

Katharina now had five sugar bunnies in her collection. She never ate any but arranged them instead on the bookshelf above her bed. There they stood, a funny little rabbit menagerie, and they were all different: one carried a sack of treats, one was standing with a garden hoe, another was pushing a wheelbarrow, the fourth was - to her amazement - riding a motorcycle, and the one from last year was sitting in a little round car.

What kind of rabbit might Frau Rosenzweig have picked out for Katharina's surprise this year? She always made a special trip into the city to the best and finest candy shops, looking for the most interesting new sugar-rabbit creation.

"Oh, thank you!" Katharina beamed as she accepted the gift. "It is so nice of you."

The post office door swung open. Herr Koeppke, whom people called "the peacock" behind his back, strutted in. He was short, but recently he had started wearing a brown uniform and high boots, very high boots, with raised heels. He knocked his thighs together in a funny way and tried to look taller. He had a moustache under his bulbous nose, and he parted his slicked-down hair on the side.

Katharina's father had been in the same class as Herr Koeppke and had said once that Herr Koeppke had always been the dumbest, an inflated zero, and had learned next to nothing in all subjects. Nor had he learned a real vocation. Under the new political leader, whom people called "der Fuehrer," some things had definitely changed. Now, men like Herr Koeppke had a vocation. That much Katharina had learned from listening in on grown-up conversations.

All of a sudden, men in brown uniforms like Herr Koeppke's became important. Everybody stepped aside on the streets and in the shops when someone like Herr Koeppke came strutting up. They all looked alike, Katharina thought, the new peacocks, even though they came in different sizes: some taller, some shorter, some fatter, some thinner.

"What is *she* doing here on Easter Saturday?" demanded Herr Koepke, confronting Frau Rosenzweig. "Now that's not what we like to see, a Jew pushing to the front of the line. Brazen, that's what they all are, these…." and he said the same words that were scribbled by Frau Rosenzweig's front door.

Katharina's heart pounded. It seemed to jump into her throat. She clasped the little package, her sugar bunny.

Frau Rosenzweig lowered her head. Why did she do that, Katharina wondered. Why did she act as if she were ashamed? This isn't right. If anyone should be ashamed, it would be the puffed-up peacock in his stupid, poo-brown uniform.

However, the peacock was far from being ashamed. He stared at Frau Rosenzweig through narrowed eyes, and she appeared to grow smaller and smaller. The others acted as though they had seen nothing and heard nothing. A woman at the head of the line turned red in the face and studied the pattern of her dress intently.

Frau Rosenzweig laid the letter back in her basket, turned around and, still with bowed head, prepared to leave.

But not before Herr Koeppke had seen the address on the letter. It was to Frau Rosenzweig's friend in France. Frau Rosenzweig had told Katharina about Paulette, a well-known French author; they had been classmates in a girls' boarding school in Switzerland. Paulette had seven cats and now and then sent something for Katharina, some little French cakes called "madeleines."

In a nasty voice, grating and loud, Herr Koeppke said, "So! Sending a letter to a hostile country? This is getting worse and worse. Apparently, you prefer the French over us Germans! Corresponding with our arch enemies? We'll soon put an end to that. You can count on us for *that*!"

He charged back and forth in his black polished high boots and stuck out his puny chicken chest.

"This is not right!" rang in Katharina's head. "Frau Rosenzweig is my friend. We talk about Sheherazade and Winnetou and Quasimodo and Esmeralda and the Nestling, and these are all *good* things! I must help her!"

But Katharina did not help. She said nothing and she did nothing. She stared holes into the knitted sweater of the woman ahead of her. Knit one, purl two, knit one, purl two.

Frau Rosenzweig left the post office in dead silence.

Katharina thought then of a picture she had seen in one of Frau Rosenzweig's books, in one of the wonderful art volumes. It was a painting of a Good Friday scene on a church altar somewhere. Lots and lots of people, dressed in medieval clothes, were mocking Christ. They were leering and jeering. Christ could barely drag himself and his heavy cross. People were laughing and spitting on him. The man in the foreground on the far left of the painting looked like Herr Koeppke, only without the side-part in his hair and without uniform and moustache.

But surely there was also a child in the painting, a girl that looked like her, like Katharina. She just hadn't looked carefully enough.

On that Easter Saturday, Katharina encountered cowardice for the first time.

WHERE IS HERR MENDELSSOHN?

E lsa never dawdled on the way to her music lesson with Herr Mendelssohn. She always looked forward to Wednesday afternoons because his house was so appealing. When she had played her piece to Herr Mendelssohn's satisfaction, there was always a slice of that delicious kuchen, which Frau Mendelssohn made especially for her every Wednesday.

"It's an Italian recipe," said Frau Mendelssohn, "handed down from my grandmother." The recipe was different from her mother's kuchen. At home, all the recipes were German.

In her parents' restaurant, the pace was always hectic and the grown-ups often pushed her aside because they were so focused on important things, as was typical for grown-ups.

There wasn't time for sitting around or reading or coloring. One always had to be doing something "useful." If you were sitting, then you should be peeling potatoes or shelling peas or knitting or sewing.

"Idleness is the devil's workshop," said her father, and a cross-stitched saying in the living room proclaimed "No pain, no gain." It was a wonder that Elsa was allowed to take piano lessons, because that could easily have been categorized as an idle pursuit. One could lead a good life without such things, things which provided no visible benefit.

But the family had inherited their piano, and besides, it looked good if the daughter of the richest people in the village was learning something "cultivated."

Every time Elsa went to the Mendelssohns', she stayed for two or three hours because they had a study full of books, among them children's books with wonderful illustrations. She loved to read, but it was frowned upon at home to just sit in one place and read. One had to be busy. Such pleasure was only available at Mendelssohns' house, which was surrounded by a most-inviting garden.

This paradise could not have been more beautiful. There was a bower of red thorn, and boxwood trees that had been pruned into a round ball and a bowling pin shape.

Huge bushes of hydrangea bloomed blue and lavender on a slope with rocky outcroppings. Next to a small grotto there were several mossy fountains with odd stone figures: dwarf-like creatures playing with dolphins that squirted water from their mouths. But the most fantastic of all was an artificial ruin, something totally English, because in 18th century England such artificial ruins were very popular, the Mendelssohns had explained to Elsa. They got the name "follies" because some people thought they were stupid or silly since they were not authentic relics from antiquity but were meant to fool people. There was even a little labyrinth such as one would see on the grounds of a very old castle.

"We saw countless castles and many labyrinths in England.," declared Frau Mendelssohn. "English gardens are the most beautiful in the whole world."

Elsa enjoyed the garden most of all in May and June, for that's when the tall perennials blossomed, along with the bushes and the early summer flowers.

"Our garden isn't just a kind of fairy-tale park; it is also a home pharmacy. We never have to go to the doctor, and my wife knows more about herbs and healing plants than anyone else in this whole region," said Herr Mendelssohn. "Birch sap is good for one's hair, and St. John's wort calms the nerves while cooked nettles are an antidote to poison and…."

"But most plants are actually poisonous, aren't they?" asked Elsa. "Laburnum, foxglove…?"

"Yes," said Frau Mendelssohn, "foxglove or digitalis. That's right. Nearly everything which heals can also kill. It depends on the correct dose." She fell silent and looked very serious. "But I know my way around with these plants. I'm a regular old potion-witch. So, not to worry."

The Mendelssohns had a special "loggia," a kind of enclosed balcony on the second floor, where they liked to sit. It was covered in wisteria vines. Every May they produced huge pale lavender blossom-clusters, almost like grapes. The Mendelssohns' house was actually a villa. They had acquired it to be their home after they both retired. Herr Mendelssohn had been a well-known concert pianist in Berlin. Frau Mendelssohn had been an acclaimed singer. They lived in Berlin and had visited all of the major cities of the world when they were on tour, so one could say that the world was their home until they retired.

The Mendelssohns could speak several languages, but they had reached a point where they just wanted to settle down in a quiet place. That's when they happened upon this house with its fairy-tale park in this little village. They had made everything even more beautiful, tasteful and fantastic. In the end, they had turned the park into an English garden and the house into a nobleman's villa.

Herr Mendelssohn was a descendant of the famous composer Felix Mendelssohn-Bartholdy, but was really just a "shirt-tail relative," as he explained, and added modestly, "and my musical talent is a poor imitation of the great talent of my forebear."

It would really not have been necessary for Herr Mendelssohn to give piano lessons in his declining years, but he had three exemplary pupils, and one of them was Elsa. The Mendelssohns had no children and no grandchildren, so perhaps they regarded Elsa as a kind of substitute granddaughter.

"When you marry, I will play, solo, the famous wedding march from *Midsummer Night's Dream*. It was composed by Felix Mendelssohn-Bartholdy." And

Herr Mendelssohn hummed the melody, which everyone knows because it is played on the church organ at every wedding. "But what am I saying? That's a long ways away - after all, you're just eleven years old. Who even knows if we'll still be around when you get married?" Herr Mendelssohn looked at his wife in an odd way, and they both lowered their eyes.

A shadow had fallen over the conversation at the Mendelssohns' coffee table in the loggia.

Embarrassed, Elsa stroked the little white dog, whose name was Puck after the imp in *Midsummer Night's Dream.*

The girl, even though she didn't really understand certain changes that had taken place recently, sensed an uneasiness and some anxiety in her gracious hosts.

"Why shouldn't you play the wedding march for me? Maybe I'll marry at eighteen - that's only seven years from now, and there is already somebody in my class who likes me."

"Well, for goodness' sake, our Elsa already has a boyfriend," said Frau Mendelssohn, acting astonished. She was trying hard to be jolly and playful.

"But it's no wonder because she has such a pretty face and such beautiful blonde hair."

Elsa blushed but then became quite pale again. She simply could not recapture the light-heartedness she had felt earlier. The mood was somber. She said her good-bye and left.

"Until next Wednesday, and I'll be counting the days. Thanks for the kuchen, the hot chocolate, and the book."

Elsa was allowed to borrow a book whenever she wanted to. She read secretly under the covers by flashlight, sometimes the night through.

"Good-bye," said the Mendelssohns. "And be sure to practice all of your pieces." Then they retreated quickly into their house.

Something was on the garden wall on the street side, something totally ugly which had not been there before the music lesson: "Death to Jews!" It had been written on the wall in bright red paint. Next to that were three huge swastikas. Elsa was frightened. Wasn't there anything she could do to stop this? These phrases, these symbols, they were starting to appear everywhere, even on posters. Elsa was truly afraid. These horrid words were meant for her friends - for the Mendelssohns!

But then she heard her best friend Gerda calling from nearby. They began playing "Balldatschen" together, bouncing a ball against the wall of the tobacco shed behind the house. For the time being, Elsa forgot the words written on the Mendelssohns' garden wall and all the other odd things which made no sense to her.

While the girls were still playing and having a good time, the community political leader, Herr Mueller, entered the business owned by Elsa's parents. The man was short like a garden dwarf, but his boots with raised heels and the funny-looking cap made him appear taller. Lately, Elsa's mother was struck by the growing number of short men (tall ones, too, of course) who showed up in uniforms like Herr Mueller's. Once they were in uniform, they talked so loud they almost screeched. Sometimes it almost sounded like a pack of barking dogs. They stomped back and forth as they talked - or rather roared - and seemed obsessed with their own importance. That's how Herr Mueller acted, a man, who, until a short time ago, had been someone of very little importance.

He planted himself in front of Elsa's mother and looked her up and down. She was a head taller, a stately, imposing woman with light blonde hair which she had braided and pinned up in a kind of crown. Her hair shone in the evening sun streaming in through the restaurant kitchen window.

The serving girl, Hedwig, sat at the big kitchen table cutting up beans, carrots and onions. She was crying - because of the onions.

Herr Mueller's rooster stance did not intimidate Elsa's mother in the least. "Are you wanting to eat dinner here?" she asked coolly. "The door to the dining room is over there."

"Not so hasty, Madame," said rooster Mueller, a bit vexed. "I do not wish to dine here even though I must admit that it smells delicious, like beef roast. I am here on official business." He strutted back and forth, glared at the serving girl, still peeling onions on the bench in the corner and weeping. He waited for his words to have the desired effect. Finally, he added, "You are curious to know what it is, right, Madame in Chief?"

Elsa's mother, whom Herr Mueller called the "Madame in Chief," was obviously unimpressed and said not a word. She folded her arms, which made her appear even taller and, by contrast, made the rooster seem even smaller. It looked so odd that the serving girl had to cover her face with her apron to stifle a giggle.

The "Madame in Chief" could not abide pretenders, which is what she called nobodies who wanted to pass themselves off as somebodies. She asked, "And just what is so important about your 'official' business'?"

Herr Mueller pursed his lips, and then he puffed out his cheeks and said, "Is it true that your lovely daughter has piano lessons every Wednesday?"

"I am hard pressed to understand what business that would be of yours," said the "Madame in Chief."

"It concerns not just me but also the Fuehrer in Berlin," he said with his lips pursed.

Elsa's mother laughed directly in Herr Mueller's face. "Stop pulling my leg. We're *that* important? That's news to me!"

"That important, yessirreeee, because your daughter takes music lessons from a Jew, from an enemy of the people!"

Elsa's mother sat down on the chimney seat behind her, but she stood up again right away. She didn't want to show any sign of weakness. The new leaders would tolerate nothing weaker than themselves. This Mueller should not have the satisfaction of intimidating her. Never, that ridiculous garden dwarf! She raised herself to her full height. She looked statuesque.

"That decision you must leave to us, where we send our daughter for piano lessons. It is our money, we can afford the best teacher for our talented child, and Herr Mendelssohn is by far the best piano teacher anywhere around. Good-bye! I have work to do. The restaurant is full. The customers are waiting for their dinner."

"You will regret those words. I shall return. We will teach you soon enough what is expected of a good German mother. I am a person of respect, and I will see to it that you comply. People who don't, well, we'll make sure that they end up where they belong. Heil Hitler!" Herr Mueller's fury made the veins in his thick neck stand out and his face was as red as a rooster's wattle. He slammed the kitchen door.

When he was gone, Elsa's mother sank down on the kitchen bench across from the serving girl. She was white as a sheet and was trembling.

"Hard times are coming for us all," was all she said. "Frightful times, believe me."

With her head held high and a smile on her face, she entered the restaurant and greeted the guests.

Two days later, the Mendelssohns' neighbor, who cleaned house for them, showed up as usual, expecting to get a list of the day's chores from Frau Mendelssohn. She came even though community political leader Mueller had lodged a complaint and was threatening to penalize her if she, a German woman, continued to "clean up after Jews."

The young neighbor liked cleaning for the Mendelssohns, who were very generous and always gave her something extra. Only yesterday Frau Mendelssohn had given her a valuable ring, which she had not wanted to accept, but Frau Mendelssohn had actually pressed it on her. "Something to remember us by," she had said to her young neighbor. "Better to give something with warm hands. They will end up empty anyway, because everything will eventually be confiscated. Take the ring; you will make us very happy, my husband and me. Where we're going, we can't take anything along."

Very strange words. The young neighbor, a sunny person by nature, had not understood what Frau Mendelssohn meant. She accepted the ring. Frau Mendelssohn gave her one more thing: a very beautiful garnet brooch which had been handed down throughout generations of her family.

On that day, the young neighbor rounded the corner and was about to climb the steps to the loggia, when she heard a pitiful whining. Puck, the little white dog, was scratching on the door and acting strangely.

The young neighbor unlocked the door and found a note on the table in the loggia: "We have left of our own accord and together, before anyone could drive us from our paradise."

In the bedroom the neighbor found the elderly couple, lying fully clothed on the bed, hands clasped.

How had Frau Mendelssohn put it? "Nearly everything which heals can also kill. It is simply a matter of the correct dose."

Elsa's Wednesday piano lesson was canceled. Sadly, she had lost part of her childhood's innocence.

THE OTHER

The door to the classroom opened with a flourish, and in swept mathematics instructor Lohmueller. He closed the door with vigor and strode to his desk on the platform in front of the class. A stout elf, so to speak. Yet he seemed to float, to hover, and still be dynamic. An unusual combination, a deceptive combination. He slammed his briefcase on the table and placed his hands on his hips.

All eyes turned in the direction of the briefcase, greasy and shabby and disreputable, but filled to bursting today. That meant that Lohmueller's hour of triumph had come because he had corrected the math test, the next to last one before graduation, and so it was time for his favorite performance.

This favorite performance, the handing back of a test, was a one-man show that was patiently tolerated every time by the math aces, who secretly made fun of him. Easy for them to remain calm. It was a different story for the others, however, on whose scales neither Pythagoras nor Adam Riese had raised a hand in blessing. Therefore, the mathematically clueless feared Lohmueller's triumphal performances. They were not among the chosen few who managed to solve "Papa" Lohmueller's cunningly crafted assignments. For them, the mathematics teacher's hour of triumph became like a prisoner's final hour, a kind of *auto da fe* (the burning of a heretic by the Spanish Inquisition).

"Papa" Lohmueller owed his nickname, which sounded like a term of endearment, to his jovial, fatherly, benevolent demeanor. A round face, somewhat fish-like eyes behind nickel-rimmed spectacles, eyes that could twinkle in a friendly way, a little round belly which indicated marital harmony, the result of nutritious home cooking lovingly prepared by a dedicated spouse. All of these things beguiled the superficial observer into thinking that he was standing opposite a kind-hearted friend of humanity.

Whoever took the trouble of studying this apparently inconspicuous man would notice sooner or later an occasional narrowing of the eyes or a pursing of the fleshy lips, which gave his whole persona an expression of craftiness and malice. Thin red-blond strands of hair hung over his forehead, in the middle of which was a bulging scar that changed color according to his dramatic mood swings, ranging from pale pink to a dark almost black violet.

Lohmueller's scar was the result of a wound inflicted during a fencing match. He had belonged to a fencing fraternity during his student years in Heidelberg. He wore his scar like a badge.

The careful observer might also have been less enthusiastic about this man after seeing him prance back and forth on his short little legs in the classroom even though he was generally well-liked among the townspeople.

"Well," said Lohmueller as he began his performance. "Well." And he tapped on his pigskin briefcase containing the fatal contents. "Now let's see who will be the taillight today." He said this in an almost kindly way while narrowing his eyes. The scar on his forehead, that betrayer of emotions, began to change color.

Wiesner, a round, healthy-looking youth with pink cheeks, son of a well-to-do master butcher and sausage-maker, turned beet red and grinned in discomfort. "No, no," Lohmueller announced. "It's not Wiesner today. Wiesner evidently studied, and it paid off. Yessir, it really did."

Wiesner beamed with joy. (If his classmates knew that he was getting help from a private tutor three times a week, they would take it out of his hide.) But the teacher announced in a loud voice, "No, no. The taillight today is Hirschfeld!" Turning toward this pupil, he said in pseudo-Yiddish, "You wass maybe a leetle crazy, huh?"

It must be admitted that Jakob Hirschfeld was a mediocre student in all subjects, but never before the taillight. The boy's handsome olive-toned face darkened with shame. Lohmueller teetered off his platform, gripping the taillight's test booklet.

"No sign of concentration, no logic, no hint of understanding. Totally atypical for your race. Your race can add, swindle, haggle, and play all kinds of tricks with numbers. What will your babba say, and your mama? 'Bad for business, bad for business!'" and Lohmueller rubbed his hands together, imitating a Jew wrapping up a deal.

His scar, that amazing scar, was changing now toward violet. Lohmueller threw Jakob Hirschfeld's test booklet at him from across the room. Hirschfeld managed to catch it without falling out of his seat. The room exploded in laughter.

"Oops!" Lohmueller was on a roll. No wonder, with such an appreciative audience. He wouldn't let go. One more shot: "He must be totally *meshugge* by now." The class was out of control. Jakob Hirschfeld sat motionless, like a statue, a lifeless nothing.

There were two pupils who did not regard this bit of theatre as a comedy and who did not participate in the general merriment. Franz Hoffmann was one of them, Joseph Stein the other. They belonged to the group which had nothing to fear from Papa Lohmueller. They had been blessed by Adam Ries, the famous 16th century mathematician, and Pythagoras, the 6th century BC Greek philosopher and mathematician, and were both at the top of their class as well as best in mathematics.

Lohmueller included other unfortunates in his scathing remarks, who, like Hirschfeld, were at odds with his beautiful and logical subject, but compared to Hirschfeld, they got off lightly. They were in a mathematical fog, but they were Aryan.

Now this benign giver of generous gifts turned his attention to the better pupils, whom he praised and to whom he handed back the test booklets with exaggerated gestures. Only Franz Hoffmann and Joseph Stein remained.

Franz was a blondish, athletic-looking young fellow with a turned-up nose and generally pleasant appearance. Papa Lohmueller heaped laurel leaves upon him. Son of a doctor, intelligence was of course inherited, it was all in the genes - one hundred percent. Everything. Yes, of course, and after graduation he was going to study engineering, good for him, yes, indeed. Germany, after enlarging its borders and was into its Thousand-Year Reign, would need engineers like him. Progress. Technology. The defense against foreign enemies. And so on. Admirable, yes indeed!

Lohmueller's hyperboles filled Franz with disgust. Without any noticeable emotion, he accepted his test booklet, which Lohmueller handed to him with exaggerated ceremony. "And now to our Number One," Lohmueller announced in a lofty tone, but in which more than a hint of scorn was evident. It was *pure* scorn. "Joseph Stein, the genius." All ears perked up. This promised to be interesting.

"The taillight and the genius. What do they have in common?" Lohmueller looked around with pleasure. One could have heard a pin drop.

"Well, Trettin, what might it be?" The girl stammered, embarrassed, "Not sure...."

"Peters?" Peters shrugged his shoulders. Lohmueller strutted back and forth. "So. You disappoint me. All of you should know this, as young German citizens. I'll tell you. It is now official. Word came today. Officially. The Aryan grandmother is missing in both cases. With Hirschfeld it was obvious. But with Stein...." Lohmueller frowned in a pretense of playful reproach. He held up his index finger in admonition.

"How can a person dare to perpetrate such a hoax on his fellow human beings? Pretending to be Catholic, and Christian...going to church every Sunday, to mass and confirmation...and Jewish all the while! Conversion is obviously of no use."

"We've been Christians for three generations," responded Joseph with calm, but a forced calm. He trembled visibly under the humiliation.

"I will tolerate no back-talk from today on and particularly none from the likes of you," screamed Lohmueller to stifle the objection once and for all.

"I will say it once more. Listen carefully, and take good notice. Beginning today, being Christian doesn't cut any ice, none. Nor does being first in the class. Nothing helps anymore, nothing! Their race is cunning, that we have to admit." He looked all around and grinned.

With a pretense of reverence, he gave Joseph Stein the test booklet and said, "And tomorrow, my son, I do not wish to see you on these premises, and not the day after tomorrow either, nor any day. Ever. From now on, our institution is only available for the education of Aryans. And Hirschfeld can stay home as well; he can help his father in their store. He is going to need a math wizard anyway because pretty soon the customers are going to stop coming."

More laughter. "And we will be an all-Aryan class."

The bell rang. The *auto da fe* was over. But then Franz Hoffmann walked up to the teacher's desk, where Lohmueller was just snapping shut the metal clasps of his pigskin briefcase. He gave the mathematics teacher his test booklet and said, "When Jakob and Joseph leave, the Thousand-Year Reign will have to forego one Aryan graduate and future engineer. I will never again set foot in this venerable institution."

The pupils, who had been fishing for their sandwiches and thermos bottles, stopped suddenly and looked straight ahead. Lohmueller's fencing scar was completely purple and swollen like a fat worm. His friendly papa-eyes narrowed. "Jew sympathizer," he hissed with hate and flew out of the room like an insulted diva.

Franz Hoffmann went to his desk, packed his compass, his pen and ink set, and his book carefully in his school bag and left the classroom. As he left, his eyes fell on the large banner hanging above the blackboard: "To the German Spirit" it read. Not very long ago it had read "To the Living Spirit."

He pondered, as he walked through the high-ceilinged corridors most likely for the last time and heard the unusually loud echo of his steps, how he would explain to his parents that their son would not graduate. He walked toward the street lined with plane trees. The way led from the wrought iron school gate out into the city, and at the end of the tunnel formed by yellowish leaves, he saw a bit of light.

THE HEIRLOOM
PEWTER

Paula had come home from school in a state of great excitement. She could hardly wait to put down her soup spoon at the end of lunch, which meant the conclusion of another school day. She did her lessons faster than usual and sent her playmates away because she had work to do.

She fetched the large laundry basket down from the loft and put it in her room. It had a cover. Then she got down to business. First, she fetched the eight large pewter plates from the display shelf in the front room. They all had the same inscription: "Karoline Ziegler, 1820." Mother had brought them into her marriage as a dowry. They had been handed down from generation to generation and were quite handsome. Then came the eight large tankards, which were also embellished and engraved. The tankards had wonderful lids, each stamped with the symbol of the stonemasons' guild and bearing the year 1844.

Paula wrapped each piece carefully in newspaper and laid them in the laundry basket. Oh, she had almost forgotten the three soup tureens. They were splendid vessels, on each of which was inscribed "May love, prosperity and contentment accompany you all your days. 1826." Paula knew the teacher would be beside himself with joy to see these treasures.

Next came the ten small pewter plates. Paula was totally absorbed in removing them from the glass cabinet (not forgetting the spoon-holder from which hung many pewter spoons...), when suddenly her mother entered the room and demanded to know what was going on.

"The teacher," Paula began.

"What is that supposed to mean, 'the teacher'?" her mother interrupted. "Has the teacher filled your head again about doing something heroic for your country and countrymen?"

"He said that we need cannons," answered Paula, "to defend our beloved Fatherland."

"Nonsense! Such utter nonsense! And so you are packing up everything to bring to the teacher - for your country and countrymen?"

Mother's voice shook with anger. But there was something else in her voice as well, a kind of panic. "Do you know what it would mean to lose our family heirlooms, which have been ours for generations? They have been used for a hundred years at baptisms, weddings, confirmations, silver wedding anniversaries, golden wedding anniversaries, even diamond wedding anniversaries - and at the funerals of many generations. And you want our beautiful pewter to be melted down and used to make cannons? You stupid, stupid thing! You know nothing."

Mother, always so controlled and proud and who rarely showed her feelings, was nearly unrecognizable in her rage. Paula felt afraid of this different mother.

"Do you know what cannons do? They tear the legs off some poor Frenchman or Englishman or a Russian or some other poor devil who would much rather have stayed home to tend his fields than to play soldier and shoot willy-nilly in all directions. Sometimes the cannons tear a soldier's arms off or even his head. No cannonballs will be produced from my soup tureens to shoot dead or make a cripple out of a healthy, peace-loving man; I don't care where he's from."

"But the teacher said that anybody who has pewter and doesn't donate it will be arrested and put in jail," replied Paula timidly. It was something to think about. She had never seen her mother like this. Her mother's words made her quite uncertain. The words of the teacher had sounded very different; he had inspired them with tales of countrymen, patriotism, the Fatherland, glory, and heroes crowned with laurel wreaths. He had said nothing about shooting off arms and legs and heads.

"Put in jail? Really! Then put me in jail. But no one will make cannons out of my pewter. That is murder, and you are an accomplice to murder, you stupid child!"

Mother's fury at the men in power, the ones who directed the war, was greater than her fear of them. Her anger came from the memory of her fiancé, who was "lost" in the First World War. This First World War had finished exactly 20 years ago, and she couldn't forget him, her dead fiancé, and she carried his picture in her heart although her husband, Paula's father, was a good man, and they respected each other and had a good life. He had achieved a certain level of financial security and status.

Her mother had received from her fiancé s comrade a report of how he "fell." The friend had witnessed his barbarous and inglorious death, how he had "died in the dirt like a dog." But Paula was ignorant of all this. She had no idea. She believed her teacher, who was what people called "a hundred percenter," someone who used terms like "countrymen" and "Fatherland" and "Yikes, yikes, let's get those Kikes!" She would have laid her hand in the fire for her teacher or jumped from a bridge. She was a very foolish girl.

Mother forbade her daughter to breathe even one word about their conversation. She picked up the heavy laundry basket, put it in the broom closet, turned the key - twice - and dropped the key into her apron pocket.

The next night one could have seen a woman digging a large hole in the garden, big enough for a laundry basket to disappear in it, and then one could have observed how she filled the hole back up, went to the compost pile, spread rich soil over the hole and, finally, strew some seeds all over it.

Fortunately, no one saw a woman in the garden that night. Otherwise, that woman could have been in very big trouble. There were so many envious people, lately also more snoopy and eavesdropping neighbors. It was a difficult, dark time, but one had to do what one could so as not to become like them. These thoughts went through the mother's head as she shoveled and seeded in the darkness. But no one saw a thing. Only Paula, naive though she was, suspected something but kept silent.

But the very next day - because news travels like wildfire - every person in the village learned that the whole pewter collection belonging to the wealthy stonecutter's family had been stolen. Also some cash, but mainly the pewter, which was very valuable and could well have been melted down to produce cannons to use against the enemy of the Fatherland. The thieves were cunning scoundrels and had managed to cover their tracks. The village police soon had to close the case; the pewter was untraceable.

That summer, the girl's mother took great delight in her sunflowers, which bloomed brighter and more proudly than ever, though war was in the air. The sunflowers bloomed all crowded together in one spot in the garden. It had the shape of a grave, or of a large laundry basket.

THE ENEMY AND
THE GIRL

Marie was no longer a child; she had become a pretty girl. The grown-ups had talked of war, and suddenly it was there. Here in the rural part of Westphalia, war still seemed quite remote. The farmers went about their chores as usual, and life in general went on as before. Except that Mother's eyes were often red from crying because her oldest brother was a soldier and had been sent to fight on the African front.

For the past month or so, the family had had one more mouth to feed: an enemy prisoner. Other families had been obliged to take in enemy prisoners. These enemies were Frenchmen, and Marie's family had a Frenchman named Charles, which meant Karl, and several men in the girl's extended family had happened to have that name, Karl.

Charles was a butcher, and for that reason he was assigned to the butcher shop and pub owned by Maria's parents. At first, the enemy prisoner was not allowed to sit at the family dinner table. A small table had been set up nearby, and that is where the enemy ate alone, slowly and in silence. The enemy prisoner learned the language of his hosts quickly, and he laughed a lot and made them laugh, too. The more German he learned, the more he made people around him laugh!

One day, the little table disappeared, and Charles sat at the big table with the family. The family consisted of a very old grandmother, the parents, the children, hired girls and young apprentices.

Whenever someone came to check on them, the little table was brought out quickly from the storage closet, and the enemy prisoner sat there, eating in silence. The minute the inspector was gone, the little table disappeared, and Charles sat once more on the corner bench at the long table, where he imitated the inspector with his red, stick-out ears and his lisp. Soon they were all guffawing.

The grandmother herself was descended from the Hugenotts and "had French blood flowing in her veins" as she expressed it with pride, and she became fond of Charles. She no longer had command of the French language the way her parents and grandparents had, but she liked to converse with Charles now and again in her somewhat broken French. This was a rare pleasure for Charles in enemy land.

One day Charles gave Marie a secret wink. That did not sit well with her. Charles knew her secret. He was the only one who knew that she had secret rendezvous with the young teacher, who had not become a soldier. He was not well and therefore had not been "drafted," as it was called.

Marie and the young teacher had been meeting for some time in the little garden shed. It was round, had lattice-work windows and a bench that curved around an iron garden table. Above the table hung an oil painting of a vase of flowers on a blue and white checked tablecloth, behind which was an open window with a view of snow-capped mountains. It was very German.

Charles had seen the two, the teacher and Marie, and that is why he winked at her. The girl's eyes said, "Don't tell." Charles nodded slightly and made some joke to distract the others. It worked. No one had noticed anything. For being an enemy, Marie thought, he is an extremely nice enemy.

Three days later Marie's mother called her to account. The neighbor lady had told her something which she did not like at all. Why had Marie chosen the milk-faced teacher of all possible suitors? And she was barely seventeen! Now Mother would watch her like a hawk and make sure this came to an end.

Marie didn't dare argue. She was an obedient girl. Her mother meant what she said and did not let her daughter out of her sight. The staff were ordered to keep an eye on her and report on the girl's every step. One time the young teacher came to the pub for a beer, but Marie had been locked in her room. She pounded on the door with her fists, but her mother came and boxed her ears.

The young teacher didn't hear the girl calling because everyone in the pub was listening to the news on the radio receiving set. There was news of victory, and the men hooted and cheered.

The next morning the mother sent Marie to the garden. The path to the garden passed by the slaughterhouse. It smelled of warm blood. Marie hated the path from the kitchen to the garden. When she was past the slaughterhouse and had come to the little kitchen where sausages were made, Charles slipped a note into her apron pocket. He winked again and whistled something softly. Behind the garden wall, Marie took the note from her apron pocket and read it greedily. The note was from the young teacher, asking her to come to the garden house at 9 o'clock that evening.

Steps sounded. They were coming closer. The girl quickly made a hole in the earth with her shoe, laid the note in it, and covered the hole. Her mother came around the corner to see what was keeping her daughter. Somehow Marie succeeded in the course of this never-ending day to slip Charles a note for the young teacher. The exchange of notes, which would have been impossible without Charles' help, continued over the next two weeks. "I am your 'pos-tillon d'amour, n'est-ce pas?'" he said.

At the end of the third week, Marie received this news: "I have been drafted after all. Farewell." The girl never saw her young teacher again.

THE ENEMY AND
THE BOY

The enemy had been with the family for four months already. The enemy was the French prisoner of war, Charles, and he worked in the butcher shop. By now he was part of the family. When the inspector came to check whether the enemy sat at a separate table, Charles remained sitting at the family table.

"This is our house, and we decide who sits at the table and who doesn't. He stays right here," the wife had said testily, adding, "He works together with us, and he eats together with us." The little folding table, at which Charles had sat for the first few days, remained in the storage closet since it was no longer needed. The inspector had left in a huff and had lisped something under his breath about "bawthy women," before lisping, "There will be repercuthionth!"

But he said this softly. Then he threw back his shoulders and marched smartly to the neighbors' place across the way; it was a farmstead, and somebody had tipped him off that a young Polish woman was working there as a forced laborer. The inspector was angry. He was told that the farm folk had actually laid a wooden floor over the flagstones in her room so that it wouldn't be so cold for her. Such nerve. Where would things end up if we started having compassion for the likes of Poles? He'd teach them a thing or two about respect.

After the inspector stomped towards the neighbors', the serving girls giggled and doubled over with laughter. The woman of the house looked severe, and the family continued eating. After the communal meal, they all went back to work. Today was the day Otto, the next-youngest son, was to begin working in the butcher shop.

Otto was less than enthusiastic. He had no desire to become a butcher. He never even eaten sausage or meat but instead kept reaching for yet another slice of kuchen. He wanted to become a baker. Or, more than that, a gardener. He loved working in the garden. Already as a little boy, he had helped his mother plant seeds. He picked out the flowers and decided where each bulb should go. The result was exemplary; no other farmers had such a splendid garden. None.

At Easter, the tulips bloomed, as did narcissus and grape hyacinth, exactly as Otto had arranged, according to height, in yellow, blue, white, violet, and light orange. In summer, delphinium, hollyhocks, goldenrod, phlox, stock and peonies bloomed in artistic groupings. Later they would be replaced row upon row by sunflowers, dahlias and asters.

More than anything, Otto wanted to become a gardener, but the war had upset everything, including Otto's plans. Otto's older brother was a soldier; maybe he wouldn't even come back - they hadn't heard from him in months. The business had to stay in the family, so there was nothing to discuss: Otto would have to become a butcher. Otto resigned himself to comply with his parents' decision.

Otto was to be trained by Charles. Both Charles and Otto enjoyed making jokes, and that made the unappealing work easier. Otto learned to add various French herbs to the sausage mixture, like marjoram, thyme and sage, and people said, "This new sausage is really very good!"

The months passed, and Otto was now nearly fifteen. Lately he had become restless and wouldn't even open up around Charles, with whom he used to share everything. One day Charles, with a cigarette behind his ear, said, "Something's bothering you. What's going on?"

Otto was evasive and didn't want to look him in the eye, but Charles wasn't joking. He said, in all seriousness, "You're tormenting yourself. I've been watching you for a while." Otto showed Charles a picture cut from the newspaper, which he had hidden in the pocket of his blue-and-white striped butcher's coat. It was the picture of a young blond SS-man, beaming and heroic, with a similarly beaming blonde girl on his arm. The girl looked up at him in admiration. Next to it was an invitation to join the German army, in this case the SS. Otto gazed with longing at the news photo.

Charles understood. Otto wanted to put himself up for hire. The "Monsieur a la Moustache" (the man with the moustache) had captured Otto's soul. Charles scratched his chin. "Mon Dieu," was all he said. He reached inside the breast pocket of his work shirt and brought out a photo. It was the picture of a boy about the same age as Otto, and he was grinning at the camera. He had a soccer ball under his arm.

"Voila! That is Jean, my son, fourteen years old. And you want to shoot at him? And at me?" Otto said nothing at all. He stared stubbornly straight ahead. Then he said, "At least, things are happening with those guys. This town is boring. Nothing ever happens here. Even the war is boring here. I have to do this job which I hate, and the adventures are happening out there." And he ran off to the garden to water his beloved flowers. Charles put the photo of his son back in his breast pocket.

That same evening a number of wounded soldiers were brought into the village, both German and French soldiers. Some of them screamed dreadfully. Three died during the night and another in the early morning hours.

At breakfast around the big table, the apprentices, serving girls, and hired hands could speak of nothing but the wounded and the dead. The war had reached the village.

Someone turned on the wireless. After some scratchy march music and *oompa-oompa- bang-bang*, they heard a shrieking voice, hoarse with anger and the zeal of hatred. It announced victory upon victory upon victory, on the Western front, on the Eastern front, everywhere.

The mother said, "Turn that thing off! It lies. We want to eat our breakfast in peace. We need our energy because, in addition to everything else, the hay harvest starts today." Later, in the sausage kitchen, Otto went over to Charles and said, "Show me the photo of your son again." It was always handy in Charles' breast pocket, the photo of his only son, Jean. He took it out. "He looks nice and friendly, your Jean. I could never aim a gun at him, and not at you either. And besides, it's not all that bad here in the village."

On that day, Charles had two cigarettes behind his ear. He offered Otto one of them. Then he tousled the boy's stiff hair. Charles said, "Yesterday you were still young and stupid." At that instant the inspector came strutting in. Charles wiggled his ears and lisped, "Tho, tho, tho..." And Otto and Charles laughed.

COCK-A-DOODLE-DO

The boy, whose name was Peter, was fascinated. He observed how Charles drank his coffee. Charles took a bowl, not a coffee cup with handle, but rather a little bowl, the kind used for desserts, and he drank something from it, something he called "coffeeolay," most likely a French word.

"That is 'café au lait,' what we drink at home," Charles explained to the boy, who looked amazed. "Half coffee, half milk. But warm milk; that is very important. You people, you drink your coffee with cold milk, but that is not practical. That way the whole thing cools off fast."

That made sense to the boy. Why didn't they do it that way in Germany when people in France were doing it? And besides, it was practical. He said as much to his mother, but her response was, "Some do it this way, and others do it that way. However you are used to doing it."

The boy's mother had raised her eyebrows, as she always did when she disapproved of something. Usually she arched her eyebrows but said nothing. She was a woman of few words, but contrary to her strict demeanor, she had a good heart and was for the most part unbiased. That Charles, poor devil, she thought to herself. He would naturally have preferred to be back home in his own country, in his village in northern France with his wife and son, running his business. Instead, here he was, working for them in their butcher shop as a prisoner of war.

From then on, she placed a bowl instead of a cup on the breakfast table and warmed milk for his "café au lait," silently and without raising her eyebrows. *Café au lait*, she said to herself, *a bit of home in a foreign land.* And every morning Charles said, "Merci, Madame."

Peter watched how Charles drank his milk-coffee. He took the bowl in both hands, raised it to his lips and blew.

"That is a *bol*," said Charles and pointed to the coffee bowl. "That's what we call our coffee cups without handles." "Why don't you talk like us?" asked Peter. "I could ask you the same question," replied Charles. "Why don't you people talk like us? That's just the way it is."

It was odd, this business of other languages. Peter had trouble grasping the notion. Apparently the grown-ups couldn't explain it either. Nor could they explain why there was war. In Peter's mind, they were dumb, these grown-ups.

Once he had wanted to know why the Germans and the French didn't understand each other, also the Germans and the English and all the rest, the Americans and the Japanese and so on, whoever they were. He received this answer, "The Germans are good, the others bad."

But Charles was good, and he was funny - even though he was a Frenchman. And some people in the village were mean and bad - even though they were Germans. What a pity that Charles wasn't German. Then he'd be good automatically, wouldn't he? But it made no sense since he was already good, so why would he prefer to be German?

Charles' language sounded so beautiful. Sometimes he sang while working, something Peter's father never did. Charles had a deep, pleasant voice. He sang mostly happy songs, but sometimes also melancholy love songs. They had to be love songs; that much Peter could sense somehow.

"By Charles Trenet and Maurice Chevalier," said Charles. Peter was only familiar with Zarah Leander, a singer with a velvety voice, and Lalle Andersen, who had made "Lili Marleen" so popular. Charles, whose sense of humor prevented him from being serious for very long, had sung once "How Can Love Be a Sin?" in a deep voice. Madame heard it and raised her eyebrows high, looking sharply first at Charles, then at the boy, before leaving the room without a word. Charles whistled the rest because it was obviously the words which displeased Madame. She could not abide this singer whom she called "Alexander."

"No woman should sing like that, it's…." She could not find the right words to describe this monstrosity of a woman singing like a man, and then such words!

Peter found that the language of the enemy (and prisoners of war were enemies; the grown-ups said so) was more beautiful than his own, which somehow sounded hard and brusque and choppy. When

Charles sang, it was beautiful, like double music: the words were already music.

The boy, meanwhile, had become familiar with Charles Trenet, Charles' favorite singer. He sang "Fleur Bleue," "Y a de la Joie," J'ai ta Main" and "Je Chante," and Peter wished to go some day to the land where people sang and talked so beautifully. But even though he was very young, he sensed that it was better to keep this wish to himself and not mention it around adults. The time was not right for praising another country and wishing to go there.

Once Charles and the boy almost got into a fight. It was early in the morning. Peter was on his way to the garden to fetch some chives for his mother. As he passed the manure pile, the rooster atop it crowed. Charles, already at work, stood in the yard and imitated the rooster: "*Cocorico.*"

The boy stopped dead in his tracks, puzzled. "That is stupid. The rooster said *Kikeriki*!" "*Cocorico,*" said Charles. "*Kikeriki,*" said Peter. Back and forth, back and forth until the boy was about to cry. "*Kikeriki*!"

Then Charles grabbed the boy and swung him up on his shoulders and said, "Sometimes he crows this way and sometimes that way, sometimes *kikeriki*, sometimes *cocorico*. I think we are both right. Listen carefully." And Peter listened carefully for the next few days.

Sure enough, Charles was right, the *kikeriki* wasn't all that clear. Maybe the French and the Germans should sit down together sometime and think about the *cocorico* versus the *kikeriki*. But it was wartime, and they had other things to do instead of arguing about words. Or agreeing about words. Too bad.

A few days later, the boy was invited to ride with Charles to fetch some wood. He was allowed to sit up front in the wagon next to Charles. They were driving through a little patch of woods when all of a sudden a cuckoo called out.

"*Coucou,*" said Charles. "*Kuckuck,*" said Peter. Then Charles said, "*Kuckuck,*" and Peter called three times, loudly, "*Coucou, coucou, coucou.*"

That sealed a great friendship between enemies, a friendship that lasted a lifetime.

THE SLAUGHTERHOUSE

The boy ran past the slaughterhouse and into the garden. The smell of warm blood rose in his nostrils. The boy could barely stand the smell. He would never get used to it. He held his breath. He would never get used to it. Never.

The war had ended a few days before. Funny, already it was as though it had all been just a bad dream. Life went on much as before. Even during the war, it had gone on pretty much as before, in the village in any case. Billeted soldiers, wounded ones, dead ones, yes, there had been those.

Now that the war was over, there still were prisoners of war, more billeted prisoners, attacks on farmers working in the field, mostly old ones and women and children, since the men hadn't returned from combat yet. Many never would.

In these new days of "peace," the damage continued: air attacks by low-flying British planes, more dead, attacks on funeral processions on their way to the cemeteries. It became a dangerous adventure to bury the dead. Now the bomb attacks were aimed at the rural communities since the cities had suffered enough.

More billeting, American and French soldiers this time. The French soldiers jumped up on the toilet seats and peed standing. They were accustomed to the "porcelain hole in the floor," people said. In France, all of the toilets were designed for either standing or squatting, said the soldiers who had been in France, on the "Western front." The poor hired girls complained about having to clean up after the Frenchmen.

Otto ran fast in an attempt to escape the fumes from the slaughterhouse. Charles was leaving today to return to France. Charles, to whom he owed his life most probably. That's the way he saw it, now that everything was over. "You silly fellow," Charles had said, "why would you volunteer to be a soldier? And you aren't even sixteen yet!"

Adventure, heroism, the smart uniforms, the companionship among comrades, real men, the variety, seeing other countries, flying in airplanes, that was always better than the boredom of the village - that is what he had thought at the time, the boy. He would probably come back with a medal, and the girls would run after him because they were so crazy about any guy who wore a uniform. And most important of all, he wouldn't have to spend his days in the slaughterhouse because this was a way out. He wouldn't have to enter his parents' business and become a butcher. Charles had talked him out of the idea of becoming a soldier. Charles had seen the battlefield, and it was worse than a slaughterhouse.

Toward the end of the war, when all was lost already, the wireless still broadcast reports of "military successes" and of "final victory" and led the listeners to believe that the world belonged to Germany. In those final days of irrational desperation, old men and young boys - still children, really - were rounded up to fight. And Otto, who had wanted to be a soldier more than anything, had nearly volunteered to go to hell.

That's when Charles had talked to him, and then he had seen the wounded ones and the dead. There was nothing heroic about them. The Siegfrieds and Hagens and Gunthers in his elementary school book had looked so attractive, especially the blond SS-men in their neat uniforms with pretty girls at their sides.

Otto just wanted to take something from the garden. He was still a gardener, deep down, his mother's best help planting, tending and harvesting. He wanted to find something in the garden for Charles to take along, but he didn't know what. Charles would be en route for days on an old bicycle. Anything from the garden would dry out. Flowers? A crazy idea. Charles' wife would take the flowers and hit him over the head with them. "German flowers, of all insulting things? Mon Dieu!" He looked at the marjoram and thyme. Charles had insisted they be planted because he liked to use them in his pâté, which he made according to a French recipe. The people in the village were suspicious at first because it wasn't German, but more and more often they ordered that "weird stuff" because it tasted so good.

He wouldn't find anything in the garden, that's for sure. But the thought sometimes means as much as the deed, he had heard someone say once. Otto liked that saying. He went back, past the slaughterhouse. He would eventually get used to the smell. He ran fast because he didn't want to miss Charles, who was taking leave today of the village, the house and the whole family.

THE VICTOR

Peter, the little boy, stood for a long time next to Charles, who was repairing an old rattly bicycle. All of a sudden he said, "Charles, it's true, isn't it, that you aren't our prisoner anymore? You are the victor, and we're the losers. You can shoot us dead now if you want to."

"I don't want to, though," said Charles, who had learned a lot of German as a prisoner of war assigned to live with this family and work as a butcher's assistant. "I don't want to shoot any of you, definitely not." He reached for his lit cigarette on the rock where he had laid it and took a couple of puffs before going back to work on the bicycle.

"People say," continued the boy, "that the victors are going to get even with us. I always listen when the men from the village talk in our pub."

"But I wasn't a prisoner. I was free to move about here at your place, and everyone was nice to me. Now I am a victor, as you say, but I'm still Charles, who wants to go home to his wife and child and house and yard. Why should I seek revenge and for what?"

Then he wiggled his ears, this Charles, until Peter laughed loudly and squealed with delight. And then Charles blew smoke rings in the air.

"Mama said that you can take our big car, the Wanderer, and drive to France in it, back home to your family. You have the authority as victor, she said."

"I don't want any authority as victor," said Charles, and he sat down on the sandstone edge of the well to rest for a moment. Fortunately, the bicycle was starting to look quite respectable, and the repairs were as good as done. He lit another cigarette; he smoked a lot.

The neighbor boy, a bit older than Peter, planted himself in front of Charles and looked up at him defiantly. "My father said the French are our arch enemies. Are you an arch enemy?"

Charles just laughed and said, "Oh là là, mon petit. Look here. Does an enemy look like this?" And he blew more smoke rings in the air and wiggled his ears. He also crossed his eyes. The neighbor boy laughed just like Peter had done. He laughed so hard he had to clutch his belly.

One of the hired girls came by with a laundry basket full of washing. Charles stood up and carried the heavy basket to the clothesline next to the garden shed. Then, after washing the grease off his hands with well water, he helped the girl hang up the wet clothes. The hired girl looked a bit uncomfortable. Charles made a gallant sweeping gesture that looked like an old-fashioned bow and sang a French song: "Sur le pont d'Avignon, on y danse…." It was a pretty song; the hired girl's face reddened a bit.

The two boys found this whole scene very entertaining. Peter's mother came through the breezeway between the house and pub carrying a second heavy basket of laundry. Again Charles helped hang up the wet things. And again he gave an old-fashioned bow full of respect and honor. It was clear that he was not trying to be funny at the expense of these women.

He sang the same song to the boy's mother: "Sur le pont…."

The otherwise serious sober woman had to smile. A pity she doesn't do that more often, thought Peter, for his mother looked at that moment so merry and relaxed, so much younger. A pity that Charles wasn't staying longer with them, he thought.

As victor, Charles would now be able to return home to his family. It wasn't far from the sea, in northern France, in a village by Arras, not far from Calais. Charles had talked a lot about his homeland, about the many beautiful bell towers built in Flemish style, the endless fields of sugar beets, the bogs and sluices, the mining towns and the little white houses with red trim. He had missed Northern France with its gritty allure, like a hidden plant in bloom.

Once Charles had said, "Most French people treat our region like a Cinderella, like an Aschenputtel, as she is called in German." And he had raved about the city of Lille, the beautiful city of the North, the city of wide open squares and of winding narrow lanes, proud and rich.

The boy's mother had to think about this. She would never see France because her work was never finished in the pub, the butcher shop, the kitchen, and everywhere else within such a large family. Through Charles, they had gained at least a glimpse of the wider world out there. He had brought a little piece of the world to her family. The boys especially would miss him, Otto and little Peter. She became serious again. "What are you doing with the bicycle?" she asked Charles.

"It was almost kaput. I fixed it up. It's for my trip home."

"But now you are the victor," she said. "You can have our car."

The boy had already said that his parents had talked about this and regarded it as a certainty that Charles would take the car, the pride of the family, for his journey home. Very few people owned a car in 1945, only a few of the "better folks" in the village. Theirs was a Wanderer.

"Non, non, I don't want the car. A bicycle suits me just fine," replied Charles. Here he turned to the two boys and struck a muscle-builder pose. "Good for arms and legs. And the whole boody."

"The whole 'body'," corrected the little boy.

"But it will take days for you to reach your village," said the mother. My goodness, she thought, such a fine man. Any other would have used this situation as victor to take the car without a second thought. It would be his entitled right.

"Doesn't matter," said Charles. "you know, Madame, my wife back home - she makes me do all the work and she issues the orders - Charles, do this, Charles do that. Oh la la, she bosses like a general...." Here he scratched his chin and grinned. "With the bicycle, I'll have a few more days of vacation."

The hired girl laughed with Charles, but the "Madame" looked at him severely. "Tsk. Charles, you are a rascal. Your poor wife. She's been doing the work of two all the while you've been here with us - tending the shop and doing the farm work!" In France, Charles had a butcher shop and a small farm.

"Vous avez raison, Madame. You are right. And I am eager to see them, ma femme et mon petit garçon. Wife and boy." He laid his hand over his heart in an exaggerated, theatrical gesture. Charles was and would remain a comedian, a joker. "But in just a few days, I will see my family."

The next day found the whole extended family gathered at the side of the road, ready to bid

Charles farewell. Most of the neighbors were there, too. Word had spread that Charles, contrary to expectations, would not be driving back to France in the Wanderer, but rather on the old rattly bicycle, which he had repaired - more or less. He would be en route for several days. They supplied him with sausages and bread. He wouldn't starve on the road.

"Charles, imitate the inspector one more time, when he came to see if you were still eating at the little folding table by yourself instead of with us," said one of the butcher apprentices. And Charles said "Achtung!" in a sharp tone, stood up straight, clicked his heels together, and strutted back and forth like a rooster, his hand raised in a Hitler salute: "Eil Eetlairrrrrr!" he said in his French accent, and the people all laughed. Some seemed truly relieved to have the whole shameful pretense behind them and discover it was now possible to make jokes about the Brown Shirts without the risk of losing their heads.

Others looked rather peevish, because they had participated with enthusiasm in all of the Hitler-promoted activities, including the goose-step marching and the masquerading. The war had ended just a few days before. People couldn't be expected to adjust overnight.

As a fitting climax to his performance, Charles wiggled his ears and lisped as the inspector had done: "Attenthion! Attenthion! Thith ith a notith from the mayor!"

After everyone had embraced him, Charles said, "Danke, merci for everything." He looked at Hasso, the family dog. He ran his fingers through Hasso's soft coat, gray with age. He was no longer trying to be funny.

He turned around, straddled the bicycle, and headed west, without looking back even once. All the family members and the villagers watched him disappear - Charles the victor, the arch enemy - until he was just a little dot where the road and the horizon became one.

THE BEST FRIEND

Never ever had Charlotte seen her mother this angry. She was beside herself with fury.

What was so upsetting about finding an old photo in a cabinet? It was a class picture from her mother's school days. It had come loose from the album and was just lying there in the drawer. Such an outburst over nothing.

Charlotte's mother was usually very quiet, almost indifferent in some situations that made Charlotte herself quite nervous. "What are you doing, snooping around in my things?" she hissed. "Why do I even still have this stupid picture? I thought I had thrown it away long ago. It's just a piece of junk from before the war."

There it was again, this "before the war."

These words lay like a barricade between Charlotte and older people. The world before the war belonged to parents and grandparents; the world after the war belonged to her, her sister, and their classmates.

Whenever children wanted to know more about the war and the years leading up to it, the response was always, "You wouldn't understand. You weren't even born yet."

You couldn't get a ticket to travel back to this era, and maybe it was a good thing. Better to concentrate on the way things were today and make no mention of "back then." The grown-ups didn't care to talk about it and exchanged glances whenever the children wanted to know exactly how it was back then, having heard rumbles about privations and horrors.

At this moment, Mother had a pinched expression on her face that was in no way kindly, and Charlotte quickly laid the photo back in the drawer. But not before stealing another quick look at it.

There, in the front row, next to the teacher, with her hair parted in the middle and wearing a suit that looked like a uniform, stood Charlotte's mother. Ten years old, and holding her hand was a pretty little girl with dark curls held by a large bow shaped like a butterfly. It seemed about to fly away. The girl looked a bit foreign. A Gypsy? Below the class, on the right, at the feet of one of the children, was a slate on which was written in the old script "Fourth Grade, 1934."

Charlotte refrained from asking her mother any questions. This was a good decision.

Mother's face, still red with anger, promised nothing positive. She slammed the drawer shut and said, "In the future, keep your hands off my photos." Then she told Charlotte to bring the towels in from the line and fold them "according to instructions."

"According to instructions" - that was one of Mother's favorite expressions. The cleaning cloth had to be wrung out "according to instructions," the silver spoon with the monogram had to be put back in the silverware chest lined in dark red satin "according to instructions," and the dishes had to be arranged to air-dry on the drain board "according to instructions."

As she was folding the laundry, Charlotte brooded all the while over her mother's inexplicable flare-up, but she simply could not figure it out.

When her mother left the house briefly to fetch milk from the neighbors across the way, Charlotte darted quickly into the living room and opened the drawer of the cabinet. There was the album. The photo was gone.

The following morning, Charlotte was the first to enter the kitchen. It was her job to blow on the glowing embers and get a fire going again. She saw something wadded up in the ash bin. It was the photo from the day before. Only a remnant of the huge hair bow and the hand which tightly clasped Mother's remained.

Before long, Charlotte forgot about the strange episode with the photo, for children can easily suppress upsetting things. Some three weeks after that incident, a former classmate of Charlotte's mother arrived for a quick visit, just time for a cup of coffee on a Sunday afternoon.

Charlotte and her younger sister shook the visitor's hand and curtsied as they had been taught. They picked out the prettiest china cups and saucers and set the table with great care.

Mother and her friend talked about old times, about their school days. At one point the name "Esther" was mentioned, and shortly thereafter the friend said, "That must have been on the day Esther was taken away."

Mother's friend faltered. She was about to add something. Charlotte noticed the hesitation. Mother had given her friend a sign, an angry motion, to say no more. Awkwardly and with obvious embarrassment, the friend cleared her throat and changed the subject. She described a cocktail recipe from America that was suddenly very popular.

Charlotte stopped listening, lost in thought. Esther...taken away...these words swirled around in her head. She simply had to solve this mystery. As luck would have it - what else could it be? - Mother developed a sudden migraine. There was no way she could walk her friend to the train station. The train was to leave at 7:10 p.m.

Charlotte offered to accompany her. On the way, she drew her mother's friend into a conversation about those early years. "What was it like then? Have you and Mother always been friends?"

"We became friends after Esther left," she explained, somewhat uncomfortably. Then she tried to change the subject. But Charlotte insisted, "Esther who?"

"Esther Rosenthal. She disappeared. Where to? Nobody knows."

"How come nobody knows? How come nobody knew? A person can't simply up and disappear."

"In those days one could," said Mother's friend almost inaudibly. "In those days, lots of people simply disappeared."

And then, sounding just like all other grown-ups, she added quickly, "But you are still too young for this. You aren't old enough to understand." Charlotte was stubborn. She was determined to learn the reason for her mother's anger. It was now or never.

"Were Esther and my mother good friends?"

"Very good friends," said Mother's friend hesitantly. "Until it was no longer allowed. Orders were orders. The teacher forbade your mother to speak to Esther and so on. The teacher had great influence over your mother. Oh well, what was the point of resisting? It was soon over for all of those people, the Rosenthals and the rest."

Then she said, with marked irritation, "You certainly have a way of worming information out of a person. You really cornered me! I don't want to talk about that period anymore. What's over is over. At some point somebody has got to call for closure. And don't say anything about our conversation to your mother about...you know."

Charlotte had heard the term "closure" fairly often of late, but closure to what? She understood little of what "it" was all about. In history class, they were just learning about the Greeks and the Romans. They wouldn't even get to the pre-war period for a long time yet. She heard rumors about it, though, from time to time. But she didn't find out about the Third Reich and all of the horrible things connected with it until years later.

Never again did she mention the half-burnt group photo to her mother, the picture in which a pretty, foreign-looking girl was holding her mother's hand. Never again.

Charlotte knew that bringing up that subject again would only unleash a new flood of anger in her mother. Sometimes it is better to "let sleeping dogs lie." It wouldn't have improved anything anyway, Charlotte knew full well, in the relationship each had with the other. Or, more accurately, in their non-relationship.

Charlotte gradually forgot about the strange incident with the photo. The years flew by, one, two, three, breathtakingly fast. She had always loved to paint and write as a child. Now, as she grew older, the urge became even stronger, this deep need to express her feelings, things never spoken, often unspeakable, to write them down, to give their silence voice.

Over and over, texts, poems and stories bubbled to the surface, begging to be put into words. She didn't even know where most of them came from. Suddenly something was there, wanting to be formulated, written down. The demands of daily life, full of small but nonetheless important obligations, had obliterated some. But the drive, the longing to communicate through the written word, only grew stronger.

A few things which she had written initially just for herself, things drawn from her innermost being, she published in small, modest volumes. Now and again she was invited to read from these books, and it gave her great pleasure to realize that she had succeeded, with these texts, in stirring something deep within other people, in touching something profound.

A married couple she knew, friends of hers, framed her modest readings in music - guitar, piano and song. The texts Charlotte read from evoked a variety of moods as some were nostalgic and happy, others full of irony or melancholy.

Once she was invited to read in a nursing home located near a beautiful wood. Many in the large audience assembled were mobility-impaired because of age and were brought to the event in wheel-chairs. Many were apathetic and most likely unable to be reached by the spoken word. However, some of the residents, mostly women, were visibly enjoying this break in their routine, and they followed the readings and songs intently. Especially the songs.

One woman in particular caught Charlotte's attention. She had come in a bit late, after the program had begun, and had taken a seat toward the back. She was probably somewhere between seventy and seventy-five, she held herself very straight when she walked, and her tanned face was framed by unusually thick, naturally wavy dark hair, cut short and with little gray. She hung on every word as Charlotte depicted the day-dream travels and the imaginary voyages of the children in her story.

The reading was over, and the residents applauded warmly. Charlotte and the musicians received bouquets of sunflowers. The attendants wheeled those in wheelchairs out of the room. The others got up slowly from their seats, unsteady on their feet.

Old age - was that really the golden years? Charlotte chose to avoid the question. It was not for her to judge.

Several of the women came over to Charlotte's table, shook her hand, and thanked her friends for their music. She knew the music had been able to move them in a deeper way than the words in her stories. Charlotte knew this and accepted it. It was amazing, really, how patiently the residents had listened when some of them were in constant pain or had other limitations.

The last one to approach Charlotte's table was the woman who had been listening with noticeably rapt attention. The one who had arrived late. She shook Charlotte's hand and said, "Thank you! I really enjoyed your stories."

She beamed and then said abruptly, "I was in Auschwitz as a child. My name is Esther Rosenthal."

Esther Rosenthal! Charlotte saw herself some 40 years earlier in the 1950's-style living room of her parents. The drawer of the cabinet stood open, "Put that picture back immediately! Who gave you permission to snoop through my things? Those are *my* photos!" Her mother's inexplicable fury. Then the singed, half-burnt photo in the ash bin next to the coal stove. Esther Rosenthal, with the big butterfly bow in her hair, holding Mother's hand.

Suddenly it all became clear to Charlotte. A veil lifted and revealed a nearly-forgotten scene. Her mother's fury back then, which Charlotte had been unable to explain - because she had taken it to be directed at her, for something *she* had done. Now it made complete sense to her. Finally, after forty years. That fury meant helplessness, shame, maybe also sorrow, for Mother must have known, have suspected, even if not with certainty, where Esther had been sent.

Now, as a grown woman, not as a girl of ten, Charlotte was finding it: closure.

Let bygones be bygones.... Others did things, too.... Orders are orders.... Is that why Charlotte's mother had let go of her friend's hand? Her mother's face years later, red with anger.

Esther Rosenthal, now the aged Esther Rosenthal, said to Charlotte, "Your stories carried me back to my childhood, to the period before Auschwitz. Everything had been so good, and then...." She fell silent. Her eyes were dry; they had cried themselves dry long ago, and there was nothing left to say.

She must have been very beautiful, this thin little old woman. Such fine features still. Her skin incredibly smooth for someone over seventy. No creases from bitterness, the likes of which Charlotte's mother already had at forty.

Charlotte said nothing. After Auschwitz, what was there left to say? *Awful, so sorry. My, how terrible. What you must have gone through!*

Better to say nothing than to recite these platitudes, which sounded like the faked concern of politicians. So she merely smiled and returned the firm handshake. "I'll come again, if they invite me back, and then you'll hear more of my stories."

Esther Rosenthal replied, "Yes, I would like that very much. The music today was lovely. My sons are musicians. One is in Hollywood!" The aide, who stood behind Frau Rosenthal, shook her head and winked at Charlotte. Esther Rosenthal, straight, not stooped, but taking tiny old-lady steps, walked to the door. "The part about Auschwitz is true all right," said the aide to Charlotte, "but not the part about Hollywood. She lives more and more in her own world, Frau Rosenthal."

Yes, the part about Auschwitz was certainly true, Charlotte thought to herself. The part about Auschwitz.

THE TWILIGHT HOUR

If Margarete had been asked, "When did your childhood end?" she could have named the year, day, and hour almost to the minute, but no one ever asked such a question.

Only she alone knew that year, that day, that hour, for the dates had engraved themselves in her consciousness forever, the moment her parents had that talk in the room next to her sick room where she lay in bed with a fever.

It wasn't being sick that ended her happy and carefree childhood. On the contrary: the illness was part of her security, for she was sick a lot with things like measles, scarlet fever, rubella – because there weren't shots for everything. It was commonplace to suffer with ailments like colds and fever and bronchitis. When she was sick, she was especially coddled and clucked over. She didn't have to go to school; she escaped, at least for a little while, her horrid math class; she was served her favorite foods. And when they let her bury herself into the pillows, Mother tucked her in cozily.

Even cod-liver oil and bitter medicine were a thousand times better than the sharp tone of the teacher and her crooked, mocking smile whenever Margarete got stuck once again in the multiplication tables. Even better, Margarete had received a box of crayons from the neighbor boy, Kurty. Really, being sick belonged to childhood and created a lovely, comfortable world, especially when one's head or throat or tummy didn't hurt quite so much anymore. It was hard not to feel rather special when one was sick, and it was especially nice to be pitied a little.

This time, on that 15th of October, 1958, Margarete was starting to feel better. The fever had gone down, and the more pleasant phase of being sick began. The next day, she would draw with the colored pencils from Kurty. She already had an idea: she would draw two girls with ponytails and layered petticoats, or better yet, how about princesses in a magic garden?

Chinese girls or girls from the Baroque period were also a possibility, the latter with large patterned fans. Princesses. She felt like a princess herself in her soft, cuddly bed, like the Princess and the Pea in Hans Christian Andersen's fairy-tale. Andersen's Fairy-Tales were the most wonderful of all.

The door to the next room was slightly ajar, and a warm light shone in to where she lay. Her parents' voices could be heard - they had been conversing for some time in the father's study. It lulled her so that she dozed off and would soon be asleep. Not only that, it was also that time of day right before dusk, for which her mother had a special name. She called it "fairy twilight." Her parents seemed to be discussing an article that had appeared in the newspaper.

Margarete never read the newspaper. She read books, books, books; she devoured them; she sank deep into the world of elephants, magicians, cursed princes, knights and beautiful maidens, of giants and monsters. One needn't be afraid, not even of witches and naughty imps, because they disappeared as soon as one closed the book and was back home again.

Her parents were talking about a newspaper article and about what grown-ups called "politics." Margarete understood not a whit on that subject.

Nor did she even care - because political things were not part of her child's world.

"That was a huge injustice," said the father. "It should not have been allowed to go that far. But we knew nothing about it at the time."

"No," said the mother. "We had no idea. None. We didn't know a thing!" Because she repeated that sentence so emphatically, it sounded as though she wanted to convince herself that she really hadn't known anything about the huge injustice.

Known about what? What did they mean, her parents? Margarete was suddenly very curious. She had started to doze off a little, but she was suddenly wide awake.

"But they told us everybody would be sent to work camps," she heard her father say. "Or they would be evacuated or sent somewhere abroad. Some of them actually did go abroad. Many of them emigrated. At least the wealthy ones." His tone was soft; he sounded subdued. "Who could blame us? We didn't know a thing."

"Yes," said her mother, "and I was still a child back then, or almost." She was fifteen years younger than Margarete's father. "We had to obey. Any objection, and you got your ears boxed," she added, to no purpose really.

Margarete no longer felt cozy and warm. She burrowed deeper among the pillows with their cheerful flower design. Her parents spoke in riddles. She honestly did not understand, only that here was a secret, an ugly secret from before her time.

"No one can judge us - we would have been sent to a concentration camp ourselves if we had raise the slightest objection."

Concentration camp, evacuated, emigrated - Margarete's thoughts were spinning with all the new, frightening words. Had her parents been aware of something? What was it? And what had they been afraid of? And of whom? Had they suspected something, though, even if they hadn't known for sure?

"The rumor later was that children were torn from their mothers' arms and shot dead on the spot. Taken from their mothers' breasts and shot! How utterly dreadful!" said her mother. "Yes, dreadful. But stop - I don't want to hear any more. Let's not talk about this anymore."

Margarete, in her warm bed, had stuck her fingers in her ears. Her eyes were open wide. She noticed that she hardly dared to breathe.

That was the moment which she later identified as the end of her childhood, the end of her lovely world, safe and unbroken. It was the 15th of October, 1958. No one ever asked her about it because it was a monumental shift that took place only inside herself.

FIVE SMALL STONES

They shot out of the earth like mushrooms in September when it is moist and warm. In southern Germany, in northern Germany, in the Alps, on the coast, in the highlands, in city and country, everywhere. The men in brown uniforms all saluted smartly and sported the same moustache worn by the Führer, "the great leader." He was the brown rat-catcher, the pied piper who beguiled, bribed, brainwashed and misled the compliant children, all with his deceptive piping.

Today Evelyn still found it incredible, so many years later, that she had followed that horrid flute player so blindly.

But at the beginning, the melody had sounded so beautiful. It was a song of friendship, of solidarity, of playing and dancing beneath the always-blue sky of the North, where she had spent her childhood and her youth.

The little pleasures had grown into large ones. Demonstrations, processions, colorful parades, and *oompa-oompa-bang-bang* every Sunday after worship in the red brick church.

A Romanesque church, the pastor had declared proudly, with a famous organ and colorfully decorated seats. Evelyn loved the little church with its hand painted walls and chancel and pulpit and organ, light-blue, white, gold, cream-colored and warm red. Most of all she liked the figures which represented different characteristics, like virtues or vices. For example, there was *temperantia*, which was Latin for "moderation" (according to the pastor). The artist had depicted this trait through a man with a pitcher pouring only a small, moderate amount into his glass.

Next to it was the representation of *vanitas* (the Latin word for vanity, the pastor had explained), a woman with blond ringlets, holding a mirror in her right hand, while at her feet a skull lay. The ultimate message was m*omento mori*, "remember that you will die," reminding viewers that the basis of vanity was transitory. Evelyn had not been able to look at this picture without getting goose bumps. It was beautiful, in a spine-chilling way.

Evelyn's confirmation class consisted of ten children. The village on the levee was small, and the names of the children were East-Frisian: Antje Harmsen, Wiebke Tjarks, Effie Matulla, Frauke Schwitters, Ubbe Appelkamp, Folcke Peters, Onno Remmers, Eicke Evers, and Inken Poppinga, as far as she could recall.

All of that was so long ago, and she hadn't been back for such a long time. Back home. She had emigrated then, no longer wishing to be happy in a country where....

She had set out for America with Ulf, her class-mate and good friend since kindergarten. Ulf re-invented himself in the New World, and together they prospered. They had been living for years now in Pueblo, Colorado, the state with the red river.

Oh, how different Colorado was from her East-Frisian homeland on the sea: prairie cacti, horses, remote neighbors, heat, and - visible in the distance - the Rocky Mountains. Her friends at the big ranch were visited at night by mountain lions and coyotes. The sea was far, far away.

At home, she had greeted the sea every morning with great enthusiasm and had walked the little path among the linden trees which led to the top of the levee where Farmer Luettge's sheep were grazing, and there they were, sometimes closer, sometimes farther away: the tides, with their ebb and flow.

That late June morning so long, long ago, she had visited the sea as usual.

The dog roses belonging to Widow Hinzen, whom everyone called "Granny Hinzen," had been especially fragrant. Clover was blossoming everywhere, along with flaming yellow dwarf gorse, pink and white yarrow, poppies and chamomile, all growing on the barren soil next to the construction rubble. So beautiful, so amazingly beautiful in fact that the scent of gorse, dog roses and clover sickened her ever since that June morning, as did the sight of poppies, yarrow and chamomile.

Fortunately, these plants did not grow in Colorado. That had made forgetting that June morning a lot easier.

On that morning, she had fetched Rebecca Katz from their shared oasis between the fragrant flowers on one side and grazing sheep and sea breeze on the other. It had been kindly Granny Hinzen, Evelyn had found out much later, who had talked to her grandson, the influential community political leader Falcko Hinzen. She had insisted that "It is high time to stop putting up with 'all those Jewish folks,' and it is shameful to have the synagogue still standing smack in the middle of town. Such an insult for every honest Christian soul, especially for a good Lutheran like myself."

Living in Colorado, Evelyn had gradually forgotten about all of that. The tang of the sea and of dog roses was hard to imagine there. But now, after all those intervening years, everything came flooding back.

Why had she chosen to return? No! Don't go to the cemetery, said a voice inside her, not to the Jewish cemetery, which - according to the attractive travel brochure - was now designated a historical monument, as was the synagogue by the village square. It had been restored to its original form several years ago.

The brochure had said that the synagogue could be visited at certain times, with a guide.

Evelyn went toward it anyway, past Granny Hinzen's quaint little house, which the villagers had fixed up and billed as a tourist attraction - an authentic, cozy East-Frisian dwelling. The same old dog roses encircled the garden. Intolerable, thought Evelyn, as disgust mixed with pain threatened to engulf her.

The little house had been transformed into a tearoom in blue and white, with lace curtains at the little leaded windows. Tea sat at the ready on the little stove, served with sugar crystals and cream in a pitcher and little silver spoons. The stove in the middle of the room had the same blue and white tiles from the 17th century: dog and cat, the protectors of hearth and home. A bird pattern, oh how pretty. The floor tiles were scrubbed spotless, as spotless as in Granny Hinzen's day, as sparkly as when the "nice" granny herself had served tea cakes to Rebecca and Evelyn, a witch in a gingerbread house, deceiving the gullible children with pretend friendliness.

Rebecca used to feed her teacakes to the ducks, which lived happily in the moat surrounding the old Frisian ruler's fortress. Once Rebecca had said to Evelyn, "Granny Hinzen, she's a phony nun. You know, like in the song of the two royal children who love each other but who remain separated because they've been deceived by a witch disguised as a nun. In the end, they both drown. Believe me, it's true!"

"Nobody is mean enough to play a trick like that," Evelyn had answered. "She is a snoop, but she's not mean." Rebecca was silent.

Now Evelyn arrived at the cemetery. A narrow path led to the place where very old tombstones with Hebraic inscriptions stood, tilting, in the grass. There was no fence around the graves, no flowers on the grave markers. Instead, there were pebbles, large and small - two, three, four, and on several, five, six, seven and more.

"*I've come back; I'll come again* - that's what the stones say in Israel. We don't have flowers for our dead. In Israel, there are more stones than flowers." That is how Rebecca had explained it to her friend back then, so many years ago.

Oh. There was the tombstone of Rebecca's uncle, Wilhelm Katz. Born 1898, died 1917. Died - that meant in this case killed in action as a German soldier in the First World War. He died for his country and countrymen. At the age of nineteen.

Rebecca's mother had often spoken to her of her favorite brother, whose name wasn't Aaron or Moses or Chaim but rather Wilhelm, after the Kaiser, whom the family looked up to. The Kaiser's picture hung in the parlor above the sofa.

None of that had mattered when they hauled off the Katz family on that hot day at the end of June.

"No two ways about it: a Jew is a Jew," the community political leader, handsome Falcko Hinzen, had declared scornfully as Rebecca's parents begged for mercy. "But we gave our son Wilhelm for the Kaiser and the Fatherland. How can you herd us like cattle now? Where are you taking us?"

"On a surprise trip," Hinzen had replied, his face twisted in a leer. How ugly a handsome face can become when expressing malice.

Many, many years later Evelyn was told what had taken place then at the county seat, before Rebecca's whole family and other families were forced up into cattle wagons. Sometimes she would awaken in the night, unable to go back to sleep before 5 a.m., after which she fell into a kind of exhausted stupor until the alarm jolted her awake. Then she lurched through the day like a zombie.

There it was: Rebecca's grave with its headstone. There must certainly be someone in her family who had been able to escape during the war years. Evelyn recalled that there had been a rich aunt in the Katz family who lived in Berlin and who had visited them once. She was plump and jolly and had a double chin and wore all kinds of jewelry. Once Rebecca had said, "Aunt Sarah has suggested that we emigrate to

America with her because she fears the worst from the new government, the brown party. But my parents and grandparents simply can't imagine that we are in any kind of danger. They consider themselves German, like everybody else. So nothing bad could happen, right?"

The aunt from Berlin had emigrated to Philadelphia with her husband and their four daughters. Certainly one of those survivors had ordered the headstone. Rebecca Katz, born 11 January 1927, died 1940 in Theresienstadt. On Rebecca's headstone lay eight small stones. Evelyn added five more, for thirteen was their favorite number, Rebecca's and hers, especially because everybody said that thirteen brought bad luck.

Several people were standing near the synagogue waiting for the next guided tour, scheduled to start in a few minutes. They looked guilty somehow, as though this were expected of them. The guilty demeanor wasn't convincing somehow.

A small group of school children stood there, too. They chattered happily, impervious to the reproachful glances of the adults. The teacher seemed embarrassed that her pupils were so unselfconscious.

Why, thought Evelyn, why this studied appearance of shock and concern? She couldn't stand those words, for they seemed so hypocritical. They were words she had encountered often of late, particularly in the German newspapers an old friend of hers sent to her in the States from time to time.

This "shock-and-concern" of the adults seemed phony and superficial. The young people seemed more honest and natural. Inner mourning needs no mask, Evelyn said to herself. I shouldn't be so self-righteous.

Oh, the night the synagogue burned, in 1938. Evelyn's father was beside himself when he came running into the house and announced, "You can't imagine what they're up to, these ruffians, this pack of vermin. They've set fire to the synagogue, these monsters. You should have seen Falcko Hinzen's face - a sneering devil's grin in the firelight. And Granny Hinzen, she was laughing like a witch and clapping her hands." Father had been white as a ghost, and he was shaking with helpless fury.

Evelyn walked by the waiting people and the nicely restored brick synagogue and climbed into her car. Her little pebbles lay on Rebecca's headstone. That was all that mattered.

GYPSY FAMILY BY THEIR COVERED WAGON

C arolin was spending a brief holiday in East-Frisia near the Netherlands border. She had looked forward to bicycling, swimming, wandering in the tidelands, but she had never before experienced so much rain, wind and cold in mid-summer. Fortunately, there were other things to do, like visit museums, castles, fortresses, churches, quaint little villages and towns of northern Germany.

In her hotel, a fortress from the 14th century and surrounded by a moat, Carolin felt a bit like the noble Fräulein Adelgundis herself. At breakfast in the ancestral hall, she sat beneath the severe gazes of stony-faced East-Frisian noblemen and their spouses. They were without exception remarkably ugly. She had time and leisure to observe her fellow guests: two elderly East-Frisian couples. The women barely spoke. The men, on the other hand, were loud, blustery, and apparently used to bullying.

There was also a trio of distinguished-looking personages, a woman and two men, all three older. They were all a source of silent amusement for Carolin.

What is more entertaining for a woman traveling alone than observing one's fellow creatures and conjecturing what their careers might be, what their standard of living might be, what kind of families they might have?

One of the East-Frisian men belched at his table and broke into some loud sailor chanteys. The genteel, dignified trio at the next table raised their eyebrows. "Such a lout," murmured one of the dignified gentlemen to his tablemates. The name of this dignified gentleman, evidently from Westphalia, was Muecking. He pursed his lips as he introduced himself to Carolin and gave his name. He was a retired judge. The other dignified gentleman, a stolid Bavarian, was dressed in black and looked as though he might be a Catholic priest. The woman, was she his housekeeper? But no, she spoke very precisely and seemed a bit conceited, so that guess was incorrect. These were Carolin's musings as she drove toward Emden in the streaming rain.

The non-stop rain curtailed all vacation options except one: the museum. But that suited Carolin just fine because she could finally study the Henri Nannen collection without feeling torn. She wandered through the rooms. The pictures had all been labeled "degenerate" by the Nazis and regarded with contempt. The artists were scorned as worthless, dabblers, crazy fools.

Paula Modersohn's touching depictions of peasant children had been ridiculed. Their faces had been described as typical of the feeble-minded, with oversized heads. Members of the SS and Nazi wives had spat upon the paintings of Emil Nolde, Otto Dix, and all the rest.

Carolin remained standing in front of two pictures that belonged together and were entitled *Gypsy Family by Their Covered Wagon*, by Otto Mueller (1926/27).

The Gypsy man, smoking a long pipe, is leaning casually against the covered wagon, The woman is sitting in the grass holding a sleeping infant in her arms.

A boy peeks out of the wagon to the right of the father. The silhouette of a small horse in the background is a black shape against the mustard yellow sky, perhaps more sulfur yellow, somehow a menacing sky. Is there an approaching thunderstorm or perhaps a greater danger? The people in the picture seemed unaware of any premonition. It is a scene of deceptive peace.

The picture to the right was a modification of the peaceful scene - the same family but arranged differently, and to the right was a laughing goat. *Yes, she is laughing*, thought Carolin.

And she recalled a certain day long ago, long, long ago.

It was before the war. Carolin was a little girl. The next-door neighbor was taking down her washing from the clotheslines in a great hurry. "Aren't you taking your wash down?" the neighbor had asked Carolin.

"Why? It's not raining, the sun is shining, and Mother said it's not going to rain either."

"But the Gypsies are close by," said the neighbor.

Just then Carolin's mother came out of the house. "No, no, it's not necessary," she said, laughing. "Who on earth would want our laundry, underwear, handkerchiefs and worn-out sheets?"

"The Gypsies snitch everything that isn't nailed down," said the neighbor sharply. Then she hissed, "Soon there will be an end to all that riffraff. The Führer is going to do a clean sweep."

Carolin and her mother went into the house. The mother shrugged her shoulders, but she looked depressed. A cloud had slid across Carolin's sunny day. "What did the neighbor lady mean," she asked her mother. "What did she mean by 'clean sweep' and 'riffraff'?"

"Oh, let's not talk about it, darling. It's not worth bothering your little head about such things," said Mother. "Come, I'll make us a nice kuchen. Do you want to help me?"

During the kuchen-making Carolin forgot about everything, the laundry, the neighbor, the mysterious words. They baked Carolin's favorite kuchen, which was known in the family as "mamakuchen" ever since Carolin as a wee child had misunderstood "marmorkuchen" (marble cake) and had thought its name was really "mamakuchen."

At noon the next day, she rode her bicycle to visit her friend Wilma. She wanted to bring her a piece of the "mamakuchen." She came to the clearing in the woods midway between her house and Wilma's.

There they were, the Gypsies, with a colorful covered wagon, a family, and a grandmother who was wearing tinkling earrings and smoking a pipe.

How funny, she said to herself, a pipe-smoking grandmother, and she laughed to herself as she thought of her own grandmother, who always looked as though she was going to her own funeral, dressed in black, buttoned up to her earlobes, wearing a big brooch and always looking pinched around the mouth. The Gypsy grandmother had put on many colorful skirts, one over the other, and she was laughing, laughing because the goat had just butted the armchair in which she sat.

Yes, right in the middle of the green space in the woods stood a wing-back armchair with the grandmother in it. From this powerful seat she ruled her empire like a queen.

Several dark-skinned children were playing a game with dice. A darkish man with cap and beard was repairing something; it looked to be a large copper kettle. And a Gypsy mother at that instant boxed the ears of a boy who looked to be Carolin's age. He must have misbehaved, for he lowered his head and sniffled audibly. Then his mother went up to him, tousled his hair, and looked forgiving. The boy looked up, and they laughed together, and all seemed forgotten. A donkey stood at the edge of the woods. There was also a horse. They both grazed as though they had a lease on all of the tranquility in the world.

"Good day," called out the toothless grandmother to Carolin. Her numerous bracelets jangled. "You are a sunshine child. I can tell that even without reading your hand. You have such fair hair, like gold, and there is much goodness in your eyes. The eyes are the most important. God keep you."

No one had ever called her a sunshine child before. "Dreamer," the teacher had called her when she wasn't paying attention during arithmetic. Sometimes her father called her "cheeky monkey." Or he may have called her "honey bun" and given her a big squeeze. That very morning the sewing teacher had called her "Fräulein Clumsy" because she had gotten her knitting into such a tangle.

Relishing the delicious thought that she was a "good luck child," Carolin rode on. She forgot all about the Gypsy family as soon as she arrived at her friend Wilma's, and they started playing with the doll house, Wilma's favorite possession.

On her way back home, Carolin came to the clearing in the woods again. "There comes the good luck child again," called the Gypsy grandmother, and Carolin waved briefly as she passed by. The boy who had had his ears boxed by his mother was playing a harmonica.

Carolin never told a single soul about her encounter with the Gypsy family, but here now, many years later, thanks to these two paintings, it was all still there. Before Carolin left the museum, she wrote something in the guest book lying open on a desk in the reception area next to the museum shop:

"My favorite pictures? The two paintings by Otto Mueller (1926/27), *Gypsy Family by Their Covered Wagon*. They show so much love, so much simple happiness. Even the goat is laughing. We know what happened soon after. The Brown Shirts sent them all to the ovens."

THE GRANDDAUGHTER

It was Agnes' fifth day in France. Her exchange partner, Suzanne, was very nice; they understood each other well.

Agnes's mother had said, "When I was a student, we didn't have any kind of exchange. It was simply unheard of even though I lived not very far from the French border. Back then, not that long after the war, around 1963, the border was literally higher than the Great Wall of China. There wasn't an actual wall, of course, I mean no real wall built of stones, but there was a wall, a border in people's minds. There was a coldness, and older people harbored a lot of resentment against their French neighbors. Your generation is so lucky not to be burdened like that."

Many of Agnes' classmates looked at things quite differently, this "being lucky." They saw the pupil exchange more like an unwelcome duty, organized by the French teacher. It required each pupil to spend almost two weeks living with a French family in France. "Exchange" was really code for missing two weeks of one's favorite soap on TV (like *Marien Manor* or *Forbidden Love*), not seeing friends, having to sleep in a strange bed, and eating weird things that were stomach-churning. There were horror stories of frog legs and an inordinate amount of garlic, of milk-coffee with a skin on it, and of other creepy things.

Above all, pupil exchange meant being courteous and cooperative without a break, saying "Merci, Madame," "Merci, Monsieur" non-stop, and having to make polite and tedious conversation with boring older people who asked lots of questions. In short, the exchange was not a treat for many pupils; it was more like a punishment.

Fortunately, Agnes was one of the few who were open to all things French, and so it was no problem for her. Her mother had told her once, "After all, your grandmother almost married a Frenchman, but it was during the war and impossible. Your grandmother's parents were dead set against it. Back then it was regarded as a scandal to marry a Frenchman."

She went on to explain that the Frenchman in love with her grandmother had been in Germany as a soldier and returned to France in 1945, but that was so long ago, she wondered why on earth she was telling Agnes all of this. "Aunt Lene told me the story in confidence. I don't even think she meant to - it just, well, slipped out."

Agnes was rather glad that her mother hadn't gone into any more detail because she wasn't really interested in those old stories. What did her grandmother's long-ago love stories have to do with her?

And now Agnes was in France. At the moment, she was listening to songs by the Negresses Vertes, Suzanne's current favorite. Agnes and Suzanne had similar tastes in many things, pop music among them.

"Tomorrow my grandfather is coming for a visit," said Suzanne. "He is very nice. I know you'll like him. He is my favorite grandfather. I call him Pépère Jean-Paul. He is Maman's father."

Oh dear, thought Agnes. More tedious conversation with boring old people; it was unavoidable. But it turned out better than expected: Pépère Jean-Paul spoke German quite well because, as Suzanne had mentioned, he had been in Germany as a soldier. So Agnes planned to speak German with him and would do her best to keep her teacher from ever finding out. The teacher always watched her pupils like a hawk to make sure they spoke French and nothing but French during their home-stay with a family. Thank goodness she was not omniscient like God.

The grandfather arrived at lunchtime. He brought his little poodle along. Agnes had already observed that the French, especially the older generation, loved their "caniche" and took them along almost everywhere.

The grandfather smoked nonstop those "coffin-nails" called Gauloises and seemed to have survived all those years of smoking quite admirably. He was, after all, over seventy. He had short-cropped silver-gray hair and animated deep-set eyes. The skin under his eyes was puffy, and he had a little round belly. Agnes liked his looks; they made her smile.

"Hello, and what is your name?" he asked in good German. He even had a hint of the same dialect that Agnes' great-aunt had spoken. She came from the Swabian-Allemanish region. When he heard Agnes' name, he raised his eyebrows in surprise. "That is not a common name in Germany," he said, again with that Swabian accent.

"Yes, it's not common, and I don't like it very much. I think it's quite old-fashioned. I'm named after my grandmother, Agnes. I never knew her; she died quite young. She died in childbirth, giving birth to my mother."

"You are very close to your grandfather?" asked Pépère Jean-Paul.

"I never had one. My mother was...born out of wedlock. And my father's father is deceased. So I have no grandfather."

Agnes knew that "out of wedlock" was something disgraceful, or at least that's how it sounded when her mother had used this expression once, long ago. She had sounded ashamed.

"Oh, I'm so sorry," said Pépère Jean-Paul. "I used to know an Agnes, during the war. It was a dreadful time...."

Pépère's funny, somewhat frog-like face that Agnes found so beguiling became all of a sudden very earnest. "I was near Schwbisch-Hall as a soldier, in a small village."

"Such a coincidence! My mother was born not far from Schwäbisch-Hall," said Agnes. "But we never go there, to Kronthal, because the relatives there don't want anything to do with us. After my grandmother died giving birth to my mother, she was raised by an aunt who lived in a tiny village near Heidelberg. That's where we live today. In Schriesheim."

Agnes didn't know why she was telling Suzanne's grandfather all of this. But in Pépère Jean-Paul's head there was sudden turmoil. It was like a movie of his life, running in reverse. It stopped between the years 1944 and '45.

Kronthal. Yes, that is where he and his Agnes had met. He had worked on a farm as a prisoner of war. He had fallen head over heels in love with her, the girl from the neighboring farm. Schriesheim, yes, that's where her older sister had moved to when she married. He remembered that Agnes and her sister Lene had been very close.

So this, beyond a doubt, was his granddaughter! And the granddaughter of his Agnes, whom the townspeople had chased through the narrow streets of Kronthal so long ago. "French whore!" they had shouted because someone had seen them embracing. The villagers had spat on her, their faces distorted with hate. No one knew she was with child. Even he had no idea.

Looking at this young Agnes, her eyes, her mouth, the way she spoke, the way she walked, her hair - he recognized her grandmother right away. *This young Agnes looks so much like her.* He had returned to France as fast as he was able once the war was over, and he had known nothing about the child she was carrying. Maybe he had not wanted to know. "What a coward you were," he said to himself.

"My grandfather liked you a lot. I could tell," said Suzanne, after her grandfather had left with his little poodle. "He kept staring at you and talking with you as though he had known you for a long time."

LONG SHADOWS

Margarete still could hardly believe it. She pinched herself in the arm so that it actually hurt. But she wasn't dreaming: it was really happening to her! She was in England.

She was in the midst of several notable firsts. It was her first time away from home on her own, her first time abroad, and in England, of all places, the country of her dreams. For years her greatest wish had been to visit her pen pal, Jane Blake, with whom she had been exchanging letters since fifth grade. The English teacher had handed out several addresses, but an official exchange program was out of the question because the war was still fresh in people's minds on both sides of the border.

There were many arguments against a visit. Margarete's parents were anxious about the safety of their only daughter. Traveling to a foreign country? And alone? Heaven forbid! So many dire things could happen. Another thing: they weren't especially well-off, and thrift had become a way of life. They were finally able to build a house, but even the thought of traveling or taking a vacation seemed frivolous and unreal.

Margarete had learned to be frugal, too. At least books were easy to obtain: she borrowed and traded many and received others as birthday or Christmas gifts. A bookworm through and through, she read books in English whenever possible and whatever came her way.

Now, as she sat in the train, on her way to Little Haywood, many sights appeared very familiar to her: houses, landscapes, villages, cities.

She recalled book titles, authors, and main characters. This little village reminded her of Miss Marples' Kindle Market. The nearby hills, encircled by overgrown hedges, were surely where Heathcliff and Cathy had run, hand in hand. A manor house with gigantic chimneys in Tudor style came into view. Its pale yellow facade gleamed through the dense old trees. A lane led to the gate house. The stately residence resembled the castle of Cedric's cantankerous grandfather in *Little Lord Fauntleroy*. It really did look like Castle Dorincourt.

Margarete could have hugged the whole world; that's how happy she was to be here. She had the feeling that she had finally come home.

At the Little Haywood train station, Jane and her parents were waiting. The grandfather had come with them, a nice-looking older gentleman who looked like an Englishman straight out of a novel. He was even wearing a bowler hat and had brought along an umbrella, just in case.

In the following days, Margarete and Jane, like two sisters who had been separated and later reunited, paid visits to all kinds of acquaintances and relatives of the Blake family.

"Today we'll visit Uncle Harry and Aunt Mildred," said Jane. They pedaled their bicycles through several small villages, uphill and down and past pubs with wonderful old names on their signs, like "The Rose and Swan," "The Jolly Farmer," "The Crown and Bell," "The King's Arms," "The Fox and Nightingale." They rode past splendid small crooked houses with giant rhododendron and hydrangea bushes in front of them.

Uncle Harry and Aunt Mildred lived in a simple little row house in Parker's Green. Next to the blue front door, a hand-painted sign proclaimed "WELCOME." Margarete was startled to see the uncle's face. One side was distorted by a horrible scar. He had only one arm and walked with a limp. She tried to hide her shock. Harry and Mildred welcomed the girls warmly, and they sat down to tea. There were delicious scones and Scottish shortbread, both baked by Aunt Mildred herself, and tea with milk, which Margarete liked more every day.

"Have you been to Germany?" Margarete asked, to make conversation.

"I haven't," answered Mildred, "but Harry has." She looked at him lovingly. "He was there as a soldier." Then Mildred, sweet and tactful to the core, changed the subject. "More tea?" Another scone?"

Of course, thought Margarete. His face and missing arm, and the injured leg, were not the result of a vehicle accident. They wanted to spare me discomfort, and so they changed the subject.

"Horrible," Margarete said. "The war. Two of my uncles died in the war, and my grandparents, my mother's parents, were killed in a bomb raid in Berlin. I...." Oh dear, what had she just blurted out? *But it was the English, the Americans and others who dropped the bombs*, she thought to herself. *They needn't give **us** all the blame.* "But *we* started the war that...." she stammered and felt her cheeks turn red.

She wanted to say something else, she didn't know what, but something to express how sorry she was, something like a confession of guilt that she was German.

But Mildred and Harry spoke quickly of other things. They needed no admission of guilt from a fifteen-year-old girl who obviously suffered from the fact that her country had indeed instigated such a horrific war.

"Oh," said Mildred suddenly, "I almost forgot to tell you that Harry and I are driving over to visit Lynne tomorrow. We want to help with final wedding preparations. Her wedding is just two weeks away. There is a lot to do, lots to organize, and Lynne wants to show me her bridal gown. I can hardly believe we have a daughter old enough to get married!"

Then, to Margarete, Aunt Mildred asked, "Have you ever heard this English saying?

Something old, something new,
Something borrowed, something blue.

The bride is supposed to wear something old, something new, something borrowed and something blue. Her dress is new, of course, her shoes are old - nobody will see them under her long dress - and her flowers are blue. She'll have a romantic bouquet of forget-me-nots. I'm supposed to bring her something borrowed, only I don't know yet what it will be."

"Would Lynne consider borrowing something from me?" asked Margarete.

"That would really be something special," said Mildred. "What did you have in mind?"

"Well, I have a lucky charm that I could lend her." She took off her silver chain with the pretty medallion that her Heidelberg grandmother had given her.

"Thank you," said Mildred. "I know Lynne will be delighted!"

Later on, Margarete said to Jane, "You have the kindest relatives! They didn't want me to feel bad about the war, so they changed the subject."

Jane replied, "Oh, let's just not think about it anymore. We live in peace time. It's 1968, and everything is totally different."

As they turned the corner to Jane's house, they saw in the distance the Blakes' neighbor trimming the hedge in his front yard. When Margarete had greeted him shortly after her arrival, he hadn't answered, and every time he had glimpsed her since, he turned away.

"He can't stand foreigners, especially Germans," Jane had explained. "He seems to have a grudge against them." That is why he was not happy to see her suddenly appear.

At that moment, Jane rode over a large stone and nearly lost control of her bicycle. "Achtung!" cried Margarete in German without thinking. "Attention!" she corrected herself a second later. Jane regained her balance, no harm done, but the neighbor straightened up immediately, clicked his heels together and bellowed "Achchtuuuung!!!" like a Nazi commandant. Then he turned to Margarete and gave a Hitler salute.

"You watch too many war movies on the telly," Jane called back to him. "My friend had nothing to do with that whole business."

The neighbor laughed a scornful laugh and yelled once again, "Achchtuuuung!!!"

A dark cloud would cover the rest of Margarete's sunny day. It didn't even help when the two girls listened to their favorite record. The Beatles, of course. *Let It Be.*

They had plans for a trip to Birmingham the following day. At the train station, Margarete was going to purchase the tickets. She paid Jane's way sometimes because Jane's parents were even less prosperous than her family. Besides that, Margarete wanted to practice her English as often as possible. The man at the ticket window perked up his ears when he heard her accent.

"French?" he asked suspiciously? With her dark hair, her page-boy hairstyle, her dark eyes and, of course, her red beret, she did look rather French, a bit like Mireille Mathieu, the famous singer.

Margarete's ancestors on her mother's side had, in actuality, come from France. Raquet was their name. Huguenots. Some French blood still coursed in Margarete's veins. "No. Not French. German," said Margaret quite matter-of-factly.

"The face behind the window looked hostile. "That's even worse," he said.

"She is my friend," said Jane and pulled a frightened-looking Margarete away quickly.

During the train ride to Birmingham, Margarete said hardly a word. Jane understood. She left Margarete alone with her thoughts. Margarete stared out the window of the train without really seeing the countryside. And the old trees of the parks and avenues cast long, long shadows.

Lilo Beil

Children's Drawings from Theresienstadt

Unending barbed wire,
a watchtower,
men with guns,
a sign with skull and cross-bones,
a tiny flower,
a little man wearing a Star of David.
His eyes are two dots,
his nose a comma,
a hyphen is his mouth.
High above: a tiny cloud,
and a most colorful butterfly.
By Anna, age 8, born March 11, 1935.
Died, Theresienstadt, January 5, 1943.

Perhaps,
Between March and May,
A camp-wide prohibition:
Drawing forbidden, effective immediately.
Pencils, paper confiscated.
You see the pictures of all those children,
you read the dates so close together:
Born - Died.
And you see your own children,
see their drawings:
the friendly vampires,
a cuddly Batman,
silly skulls and crossbones,

goofy devils.
And the real horror drives you toward the exit.
        --Lilo Beil

(Prague, Spring 1989, an exhibition in the Jewish quarter)

Parental Love, 1939, or The Friendly Hangman

Men to the left, women to the right,
children straight ahead.
But be quick about it,
or I'll make you sorry.
He cracks his whip;
by 5 o'clock order reigns.
End of shift.
The hangman heads for home.

Soup steams on the table.
He stretches comfortably in his easy chair,
and reads the *People's Observer*
(den Völkischen Beobachter).

He strokes his son's blond hair
and pinches his wife's backside.
Sometimes, in the night, he hears screams:
pleading mothers, sobbing children, desperate fathers.
Mama, where are you? --No, not my child!
He wakes up sweating.
But orders are orders.

He has pulled the early shift.
And gently,
oh so gently
he glides out the door
so as not to wake his child.

--Lilo Beil, 1990

STORY NOTES

SHADOW TIME
No specific background material exists for this introductory story of *Shadow Time*. In it I try to make real the era in which the rest of the stories occur.

THE SAILOR DRESS
This is my mother's story. I was shocked when she told me that she never wore the sailor dress. Uncle Rudolf was my father's eldest brother. He emigrated to America around 1905. When he visited his family in the Palatinate, he was already very sick and died soon after his return to America in 1937 or '38. He had said, "There will be war," but nobody believed him at the time.

LEA'S JOURNEY TO THE EAST
This story was inspired by a ballet performance in which my young daughter Johanna danced the part

of the sugar plum fairy. I imagined how it might have been, had Johanna lived in that era and if she had had a dear friend who was Jewish.

WHEN THEY KILLED THE CHRIST CHILD
For this story, I imagined how it might have been if I as a pastor's daughter had been alive during the Third Reich instead of being born after the war. What dilemmas might I have had to face?

THE SUGAR BUNNY
This story was told to me by the school secretary, Emma Bickel. She wept as she described her "cowardice" in the post office. The Jewish lady's name was Frau Marx.

WHERE IS HERR MENDELSSOHN?
There is no specific background for this story. It came entirely out of my imagination.

THE OTHER
My daughter Johanna had a friend whose grandfather was "The Other." This friend told me about him, and I was impressed and inspired. There were, indeed, courageous Germans who actively resisted, but almost all of them were put to death. The young fellow in this story was lucky.

THE HEIRLOOM PEWTER

The mother in this story was my grandmother Elsa Knapp, and the "stupid child" was my mother. Her teacher was an authentic Nazified teacher - as in "The Sailor Dress."

THE ENEMY AND THE GIRL, THE ENEMY AND THE BOY, COCKADOODLE-DOO, THE SLAUGHTERHOUSE, AND THE VICTOR

These five stories are based on anecdotes recounted by my mother about the French prisoner of war who was billeted with her family because they had a large farm with a butchering operation and an inn, and he was a butcher/sausage-maker back in Normandy [northern France]. The prisoner's name was Hubert Lévêque; I call him Charles in these stories. He worked until the end of the war for my grandparents, Wilhelm and Elsa Knapp, and was treated not as an enemy but as a friend.

The friendship exists still today between us and Hubert Lévêque s son and daughter-in law, Jean and Denise Lévêque [now in their 80's], who live in northern France. The father, Hubert, died long ago. He, by the way, played cupid at one point and convinced my grandparents that my father and mother should marry.

THE BEST FRIEND
After a reading of my stories at a retirement facility in the Odenwald north of Heidelberg, this actually happened to me: a resident came up to me and related that she had been in imprisoned in the Auschwitz concentration camp near Krakow, Poland. She was beginning to suffer dementia and had no son in Hollywood, nor was she the best friend of my mother, as in the story. It is easy to see where fact and fiction begin to intermingle. In the end, it does not matter, does it? I mean, for the story itself to speak to its readers....

THE TWILIGHT HOUR
The little girl who overhears her parents talking and learns for the very first time about the Holocaust was...me! I have never recovered from this dismay.

FIVE SMALL STONES
Many years ago I took a trip to northern Germany by myself. In the town where I stayed, there was a synagogue and a Jewish cemetery. The "cozy" atmosphere of the town seemed quite at odds with the scenes which must have played out during the deportation of Jews to the concentration camps.

"GYPSY FAMILY BY THEIR COVERED WAGON"
When I was alone on holiday in Northern Germany, I visited the museum in Emden and saw a painting called *Gypsy Family by Their Covered Wagon*. It

was painted by Otto Müller, who, by the way, was himself a Gypsy. Nowadays they are more correctly called either Sinti or Roma. I was deeply moved by what I saw in the picture and discovered that I was crying.

THE GRANDDAUGHTER
My experiences as a French teacher helped to inform this story. I accompanied my French classes to France many times for home-stays. This actual story is based on speculation. It is well known that German girls and women who had love relationships with prisoners of war were publicly shamed as whores. The same fate befell French women and girls who fell in love with German soldiers. Their heads were shaved and they were chased through the streets, struck and spat upon. Any children resulting from these relationships were openly called bastards and treated with contempt.

LONG SHADOWS
I had an unpleasant experience in England when I was there with my husband and young daughters. As we arrived to visit acquaintances of our friend Mary, one of our daughters stumbled on the steps. Instinctively, I called out "Achtung!" (which can mean either "Watch out!" or "Attention!"). The host drew himself stiffly in front of me, saluted like a Nazi and said, "Achtung!" in a cynical tone. I was very

hurt. He was one of those who watched too many war movies and deduced that all Germans were Nazis. It was stupid, but stupidity hurts, too.

Children's Drawings from Theresienstadt
My husband and I were in Prague with friends in 1987. We visited the Holocaust museum in the Jewish Quarter and saw the exhibit of children's drawings from Theresienstadt. Theresienstadt was a concentration camp for women, children and old people. The exhibit featured pictures drawn and/or painted by Jewish children who were in the same age group (5-8) as my own three daughters. I imagined what it would be like if *they* had made these pictures – and I ran outside in tears. A few weeks later I got up in the middle of the night and wrote this poem.

Parental Love, 1939, or The Friendly Hangman
This poem was not triggered by a single event like going to the exhibition in Prague, but over the years I have been aghast when reading about those "little cogs in the wheel," those people who functioned like automatons, those overseers in the camps who tortured people and at the same time were good fathers and husbands, and who treated their pets lovingly. This is what Hannah Arendt called "the banality of evil," mentioned in my introduction to this book: dreadful acts carried out by "normal" people.

ABOUT THE AUTHOR

Lilo Beil, née Seiferling, was born in 1947 in Klingenmuenster (Landkreis Southern Weinstrasse) and spent her childhood and youth in a parsonage in the town of Winden. She attended the Progymnasium in Bad Bergzabern and the Modern Language Gymnasium in Landau (today the Max Slevogt Gymnasium*), from which she graduated in 1966.

After studying English and French in Heidelberg, she taught those languages at the Martin Luther Schule, a Gymnasium* in the town of Rimbach/Odenwald, located north of Heidelberg and south of Frankfurt. She and her husband, a former teacher and an antiques evaluator, live in the area. They have three grown daughters and a grandson. She is retired and now writes full-time.

Publications: *Maikaefersommer* (*Lightningbug Summer: A Childhood in the Palatinate in the 1950's*) (*1997*); *Sonnenblumenreise* (*Sunflower Travels: Stories for Travelers and Non-Travelers*) (*1999*); *Heute Kein Spaziergang* (*No Walk Today: Detective Stories of Love, Art and Death* (*2002*); also poems, satire and short stories in various German anthologies. In 2013 *Mord auf Vier Pfoten* (*Murder on Four Paws*) appeared. It consists of 22 mystery stories for animal lovers.

Lilo Beil is the author of a popular series of whodunit novels featuring Inspector Friedrich Gontard. They all deal with events in Germany's history or with current social problems.

Schattenzeit was published in Germany in 2005 by Tintenfass Verlag (Inkwell Press). and was translated by Virginia Larsen of Austin, Minnesota. Virginia Larsen also taught at the Martin Luther Schule/ Gymnasium*.

Lilo Beil welcomes responses and questions from readers. She can be contacted via her website www. lilobeil.de.

Gymnasium is the equivalent of a college-preparatory high school.

34603166R00098

Made in the USA
San Bernardino, CA
03 June 2016